Health Awareness & English Conversation

New Edition

Healthtalk

Bert McBean

Tryalogue
Education

はじめに

　この専門的なテキストは、日本の学生のみなさんが健康に対する意識を高め、同時に英会話の練習教材として利用するという2つの大きな目的で書かれています。

　またワークブックとしての役割もあり、学生のみなさんが中心となってコミュニケーションをするためのテキストでもあります。「聞く」「話す」「読む」「書く」の4つの基本技能が身につけられるようになっていますが、特に「聞く」「話す」に重点が置かれています。出版社のウェブサイトよりオーディオファイルをダウンロードすることもできます。

　HEALTHTALK は、中級レベルの若い英語学習者のための教科書です。内容は少し堅苦しく感じられるかもしれませんが、ユーモア溢れるイラストや対話によって分かりやすい内容となっています。重要な健康に関する知識は強調され、繰り返し触れられています。馴染みのない健康に関する単語や表現は、巻末に掲載されています。

　本書が最初に出版されて以来、時代の変化とともに医学的な新たなデータや情報が発表され、それに伴いこのテキストも改訂され内容も更新されてきました。

　本書は、「健康に関する意識チェック表」に記入することからテキストが始まります。テキストの内容に沿った簡単な12の質問に答えるようになっており、学習する前のチェック表の結果と、学習後のチェック表の結果を比べることで、どのくらい健康に関する意識が改善されたかがわかるようになっています。

　このテキストを読んだ学生のみなさんの中に、自分の健康について考え、たとえば禁煙をしたり、歯科チェックを受けるようになる人が一人でもいれば、*HEALTHTALK* はその目的の一つを達成したことになるでしょう。

著　者

Preface

This content-based textbook has two important aims: to increase the health awareness of Japanese students, and, at the same time, to give them practice in English conversation.

The text, which also functions as a workbook, is communicative and student-centered. It develops the four skills of listening, speaking, reading, and writing, with the emphasis on listening and speaking. It is supplemented by audio files, which are available on the publisher's web site.

HEALTHTALK is for young adults at the intermediate level. The material is presented in a serious, authoritative style, yet humorous illustrations and dialogues give it a lighthearted touch. Important health points are stressed and reiterated throughout the lessons. Because a number of uncommon health-related words and expressions appear, an English-Japanese glossary is included in the back of the book.

Since the initial publication of this text, new data and information have continually surfaced on the topics presented. The original data and information have been revised and updated accordingly.

Two identical health-awareness check sheets was added in the last edition. Each is a simple set of twelve key questions, one from each unit in the text. The before-the-course check sheet is intended to show students how little they know about good health habits. The same check sheet taken at the end of the course will, hopefully, show students how much their health awareness has improved as a result of having studied the textbook.

If even a few students, after reading this book, think more about their health—whether it be quitting smoking or getting a dental checkup—*HEALTHTALK* will have met one of the aims for which it was written.

Bert McBean

Contents

MY HEALTH AWARENESS CHECKSHEET

Name		Number		Date	

I know… *Circle Yes or No*

1	the four things that cause people to die early.	Yes	No
2	what percentage of all cancers is related to lifestyle.	Yes	No
3	how many minutes each cigarette shortens a smoker's life.	Yes	No
4	what percentage of Japan's garbage comes from packaging.	Yes	No
5	how many minutes a week I should exercise.	Yes	No
6	what "junk food" means.	Yes	No
7	the two problems that alcohol causes.	Yes	No
8	what problems severe stress can cause in my body.	Yes	No
9	what BMI means.	Yes	No
10	how many teeth the average person has.	Yes	No
11	where I can get a free HIV/AIDS test in Japan.	Yes	No
12	how to determine whether or not a person has depression.	Yes	No

MY SCORE: *Circle One*

9–12 <u>Yes</u> answers: My health awareness level is .... HIGH ☺

5–8 <u>Yes</u> answers: My health awareness level is .... SO-SO 😐

1–4 <u>Yes</u> answers: My health awareness level is .... LOW ☹

MY HEALTH AWARENESS CHECKSHEET: RESULT

Name		Number		Date	

I know...   *Check Yes or No*

1	the four things that cause people to die early. (Page 2)	Yes	No
2	what percentage of all cancers is related to lifestyle. (14)	Yes	No
3	how many minutes each cigarette shortens a smoker's life. (26)	Yes	No
4	what percentage of Japan's garbage comes from packaging. (38)	Yes	No
5	how many minutes a week I should exercise. (50)	Yes	No
6	what "junk food" means. (62)	Yes	No
7	the two problems that alcohol causes. (74)	Yes	No
8	what problems severe stress can cause in my body. (86)	Yes	No
9	what BMI means. (98)	Yes	No
10	how many teeth the average person has. (110)	Yes	No
11	where I can get a free HIV/AIDS test in Japan. (122)	Yes	No
12	how to determine whether or not a person has depression. (134)	Yes	No

My number of **yes** answers at the end of the course, Page vii.   (   )

My number of **yes** answers from the start of the course, Page vi.   — (   )

Plus no: ☐

MY RESULTS: *Circle One*

My health awareness level has .... IMPROVED A LOT ▲▲

My health awareness level has .... IMPROVED A LITTLE ▲

My health awareness level has .... NOT IMPROVED ▼

 02

You Can Live to Be a Hundred

Scientists say our bodies are designed to last 100 years. Yet, most people die before 100. Why? One reason is that people don't think enough about health. Although none of us know how long we will live, there are certain things that lengthen or shorten a person's life. They are your gender (male or female), personality, success, family background, lifestyle, and health. In this book, we will focus on the last two since we can control them.

As for health and lifestyle, there are four main things that cause people to die early—usually before the age of 85:

- Lack of Exercise
- Tobacco Smoking
- Obesity
- Unhealthy Diet

Therefore, to live a long life and improve the quality of your life today, you should eat good food, keep your weight down, exercise, and not smoke. 15

But, that's not all. You also need to live a balanced life. For example, you need just so much of certain types of food. You need just the right amount of exercise, sleep, and relief from stress.

You may think living a healthy life is simple. It isn't, because it requires effort and willpower. Consider foods, for example. Can you give up po- 20 tato chips, candy, and other "junk food"? They taste great. Unfortunately, they're not healthy foods; they're worthless calories. How about exercise? It's difficult to keep up a regular training program, to do an exercise at least three times a week that gives the lungs, heart, and muscles a good workout. Another problem is stress; there is a lot of it in society today. 25 Finally, add in all the bad habits that people have like smoking, drinking, and not eating breakfast, and you can understand why keeping a healthy lifestyle is so difficult. It is understandable why so few people live to be 100 years old, even with the advances in modern medicine which have increased average life spans. Japan is near the top in life expectancy, but 30 this may change as lifestyles change.

Cancer, heart disease, and stroke, which affects blood flow to the brain, account for about 60 percent of all deaths in Japan. These are mainly lifestyle diseases caused by people's diet and behavior.

Keeping a positive attitude can also help you live longer. Scientists have 35 found that positive thinking can add about eight years to your life. You can't control everything that happens to you in your life, but you do have control over how you react to things. Try to look at the good side of life.

Wait a minute! You say you don't care about living to 100; you say an average life span is enough? However, wouldn't you like to have more 40 energy, prettier teeth, more self-confidence, be more handsome or more beautiful and avoid cancer as long as you live? Of course you would. And you can. This textbook is your guide to a long, healthy life. Just read it, believe it, and do it. Oh, one more thing: don't forget to fasten your seatbelt! 45

Five Questions Plus One

Answer the five questions. Then, make a question to be written on the blackboard for the class to answer.

① What is one reason most people die before age 100?

② What two things will this textbook focus on?

③ What is this textbook a guide to?

④ What are some bad habits that people have?

⑤ Why isn't it simple to live a healthy lifestyle?

Plus One

Your Question: _____

The Answer: _____

True or False Questions

Circle T (True) or F (False) for each statement. If the statement is False, rewrite it to make it True.

T F **1.** You can't do anything about changing your sex or family background.

T F **2.** You do have control over your health and lifestyle.

T F **3.** A healthy lifestyle takes little effort.

T F **4.** Cancer can never be prevented.

T F **5.** On the average, men live seven years longer than women.

Getting Information

You can get a general idea of how long you will live by filling in the questionnaire below.

Answer the questions for yourself and add or subtract points as indicated if your answer is "yes." Do it again with your partner.

How Long Will You Live?

		You	Partner
1. Your Sex (gender)	**STARTING AGE**	78	78
a. Are you a man?	(If "yes") − 2 (	) (	)
b. Are you a woman?	(If "yes") + 4 (	) (	)
2. Lifestyle			
a. Do you live in a big city (over two million)?	− 3 (	) (	)
b. Do you live in a small town (under 10,000)?	+ 2 (	) (	)
c. Do you usually work at a desk?	− 3 (	) (	)
d. Does your work require physical activity?	+ 3 (	) (	)
e. Do you exercise at least three times a week for 30 minutes?	+ 2 (	) (	)
f. Do you live with someone?	+ 5 (	) (	)
g. Do you live alone?	− 1 (	) (	)
3. Personality			
a. Do you sleep more than 10 hours a night?	− 4 (	) (	)
b. Do you sleep less than five hours a night?	− 4 (	) (	)
c. Are you always in a hurry?	− 3 (	) (	)
d. Are you usually easygoing and relaxed?	+ 3 (	) (	)
e. Are you happy most of the time?	+ 1 (	) (	)
f. Are you unhappy most of the time?	− 2 (	) (	)
4. Success			
a. Are you a college student or college graduate?	+ 1 (	) (	)
b. Will you or did you get a master's degree?	+ 2 (	) (	)

5. Family Background

a. Have any of your grandparents lived to age 85?

+ 2 ( ) ( )

b. Have all four of your grandparents lived to age 80?

+ 6 ( ) ( )

c. Has either of your parents died of a heart attack before age 50?

– 4 ( ) ( )

d. Has any parent, brother, or sister had heart disease or diabetes?

– 3 ( ) ( )

6. Health Habits

a. Do you smoke two or more packs of cigarettes a day?

– 10 ( ) ( )

b. Do you smoke one pack of cigarettes a day? – 7 ( ) ( )

c. Do you smoke a half pack of cigarettes a day? – 5 ( ) ( )

d. Are you overweight by seven kilograms?* – 2 ( ) ( )

e. Are you overweight by three kilograms?* – 1 ( ) ( )

*Check this on page 113.

f. Do you have a medical check every year? + 2 ( ) ( )

Age adjustment for persons over 30 years old: if you are
31–40, add 2;
41–50, add 3;
51–70, add 4 to the total.

TOTAL YEARS ( ) ( )

You   Partner

What is your partner's name? _____

How long can he/she expect to live? _____

How long can you expect to live? _____

What can you do to live longer? _____

What is your target age? (circle)   70   75   80   85   90   95   100

Go for it by living a healthy lifestyle!

Matching for Understanding

Choose the expression on the right that means the same as the word on the left, as it is used in the text.

1. design   (   )   **a.** something done regularly

2. habit   (   )   **b.** trying very hard

3. last   (   )   **c.** not enough

4. lifestyle   (   )   **d.** having no value

5. obesity   (   )   **e.** feeling good about yourself

6. effort   (   )   **f.** put on; connect

7. willpower   (   )   **g.** the kind of life you live

8. worthless   (   )   **h.** energy used by the body

9. lungs   (   )   **i.** not wear out

10. calorie   (   )   **j.** they pass air into blood

11. confidence   (   )   **k.** plan or make

12. simple   (   )   **l.** being overweight

13. scientists   (   )   **m.** strong desire

14. lack of   (   )   **n.** researchers

15. fasten   (   )   **o.** easy

 *Dialogue Dictation* 03

Fred is telling John about a strange race in which he lost $85 on a bet. Listen and write the missing words.

Fred: When I was _____, I met an _____

_____ who wanted to _____.

John: How _____ was _____?

Fred: He _____ like _____ was about _____.

John: You are _____, so you _____ have been

_____ than _____.

Fred: That's _____ I thought. So, I _____ to

_____ for _____.

John: How _____ did _____ bet?

Fred: One _____ for each _____ difference in

_____ _____.

John: Did you _____ the _____ and get

$_____?

Fred: No, I _____ eighty-_____ dollars.

John: Why _____ you _____ so _____?

Fred: Well, _____ I found _____ he was

_____ 105 _____ old!

↻ *Check your answers by using the* **Dialogue Practice** *page.*

Dialogue Practice

1. Read; 2. Remember; 3. Look Up; and 4. Speak. After you finish, change roles and do it again.

A

Fred: ....
....

John: How **old** was **he**?

Fred: ....

John: You are **20**, so you **should** have been **faster** than **him**.

Fred: ....
....

John: How **much** did **you** bet?

Fred: ....
....

John: Did you **win** the **race** and get **$50**?

Fred: ....

John: Why **did** you **lose** so **much**?

Fred: ....
....

B

Fred: When I was **jogging**, I met an **old man** who wanted to **race**.

John: ....

Fred: He **looked** like **he** was about **70**.

John: ....
....

Fred: That's **what** I thought. So, I **agreed** to **race** for **money**.

John: ....

Fred: One **dollar** for each **year's** difference in **our ages**.

John: ....

Fred: No, I **lost** eighty-**five** dollars.

John: ....

Fred: Well, **later** I found **out** he was **actually** 105 **years** old!

 You and Your Partner

Palm Reading:
Predict Your Partner's Future

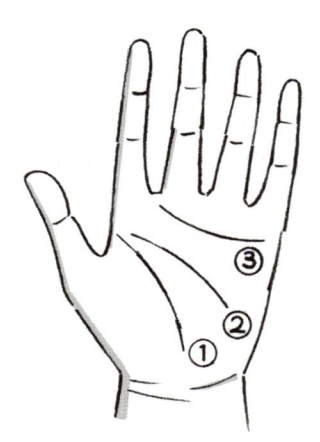

Palm reading is a mysterious art. It is a way
of making predictions about a person's future.
Look at the three main lines in the picture,
then find them on your hand.

Line	Long	Short
1. LIFE LINE	You will live a long life.	You had better watch your lifestyle.
2. HEAD LINE	You will be smart and successful.	You will have to study and work harder.
3. HEART LINE	You will easily find romance.	You may have a hard time finding a girlfriend or boyfriend.

Next, read your partner's palm and make predictions like this:

1. Your LIFE LINE is _____, so _____.

2. Your HEAD LINE is _____, so _____.

3. Your HEART LINE is _____, so _____.

Do you agree or disagree with each prediction? Why?

1. agree/disagree *Reason:* _____.

2. agree/disagree *Reason:* _____.

3. agree/disagree *Reason:* _____.

Finally, make one funny prediction to tell your partner. For example, "You
are a handsome boy, so I predict you will marry a rich girl."

Prediction: _____

Read This

How You Grow Old

BRAIN POWER
Nerve cells die and memory begins to fail.

IMMUNE SYSTEM
Defense against disease drops by 20 percent in old age.

SIGHT
After middle age, it becomes difficult to read small print.

HEARING
Hearing loss is common in old age, especially at high frequencies.

TEETH
Rates of gum disease, oral cancer, and cavities increase.

SKIN
By age 50, skin sags and becomes wrinkled and rough.

HEART
The heart weakens and pumping power drops 30% by age 70.

LUNGS
Breathing capacity declines 0.8 percent per year from age 20 to 70.

MUSCLES
Muscles weaken and some muscle is lost.

POSTURE
The body tends to become stooped in old age.

BODY FAT
It redistributes from under the skin to deeper parts of the body. (Metabolic Syndrome)

BONES
By age 40, people begin to lose bone tissue.

You can slow down the aging process with good health habits.

Question: What happens to your _____ when you get old?

Answer: _____

 **Listening for Content** 04

Read, listen, and then write to complete the sentences.

Why Japanese Live Longer than Americans

The Japanese live longer than any other people in the world. Here are the average years a baby born today will live in Japan and in the U.S.A.:

	Japan	U.S.A.
Average	83	78

(Figures are approximate.)

Experts believe the reason is the difference in diet:

1. The Japanese _____ is _____ in _____ and

_____, and _____ in _____.

2. This is _____ they _____ a lot of _____,

_____, fresh _____, and _____.

3. As a _____, cholesterol and _____ disease

_____ are _____.

4. However, the _____ diet is _____ yearly.

5. It is becoming _____, and _____ are eating

_____ products, _____, and so on.

6. Experts _____ that if the _____ continues to

_____, life spans will _____ to _____.

Activities for Conversation Practice

A Agree or Disagree

What is your opinion of the following statement? Make notes in the appropriate box and get ready to give your reasons when asked by your teacher or your partner.

> **All "junk food" should hve warning labels on it.**

AGREE	DISAGREE

B Create a Dialogue

One student be A and the other be B. Work together and write out five exchanges of at least five words each. Practice; then do the dialogue in front of the class.

1. **A** is 84 years old and is living alone. **A**'s son, **B**, wants to put his father in a lodging home. The father refuses to go.

2. **A** wants to visit a palm reader because he is going to get married. His girlfriend, **B**, thinks seeing a palm reader is a bad idea.

3. **A** wants to know his girlfriend's, **B**'s, true age (she is 30). He asks her many questions to learn her age, but she gives wrong answers to confuse him.

C Topics for Discussion and Writing

Individual and group. Write out your answers for the following questions, then discuss them with your classmates.

1. Japanese live longer than Americans. Why do you think this is so?

2. Who is the oldest person you know? Tell about that person.

3. The number of Japanese who are over 100 years old is more than 50,000. Of the total, about 80 percent are women. Why do you think women live longer than men?

🎧 05

Ten Ways to Prevent Cancer

Cancer became the number one cause of death in Japan in 1981, and it has increased every year since. These days, about 30 percent of all deaths are due to cancer. In fact, about every two minutes someone in Japan dies of cancer. Maybe that's why just hearing the word "cancer" scares most
5 people. Some think cancer is like a terrible lottery: you're unlucky if you get it and lucky if you don't. That way of thinking is wrong.

It's okay to be afraid of the disease, but it's wrong to feel helpless about it because 80–85 percent of all cancers are related to lifestyle—the way you live your life. For example, the food you eat, the amount of stress in
10 your life, and whether you smoke or not, affect your chances of getting cancer.

Here is a list of five important things you can do every day to protect yourself from cancer:

EAT HIGH-FIBER FOODS

Foods that are high in fiber such as fruit, vegetables, and whole grains 15
can prevent colon cancer. Some common whole grain foods are whole
wheat (brown) bread, whole grain (brown) rice, and oatmeal.

REDUCE FAT IN YOUR MEALS

Too much fat in food increases the chance of breast, colon, and
prostate cancer. Eat fewer foods cooked in fat and oil; eat more lean 20
meat, fish, and low-fat dairy products.

CONTROL YOUR WEIGHT

A study found that men who were 40 percent or more overweight
had a 33 percent greater chance of getting cancer than people who
were not fat. 25

AVOID NITRITE-CURED FOODS

These types of foods include ham, bacon, hot dogs, and sausage.
They may cause stomach cancer.

DON'T SMOKE CIGARETTES

About 30 percent of all cancer is clearly because of cigarette smoking. 30
People who smoke have a 15-times greater chance of getting cancer
than those who don't.

Some other things you can do to avoid cancer are these: get plenty
of vitamins A and C; eat more green vegetables; don't drink too much
alcohol; avoid too much sun; think positively in your daily life. 35
Although your chances of getting cancer increase as you get older,
nearly half of all cancer patients can be cured by modern medicine.
Now you can understand why cancer is related to lifestyle, and you
know some ways to help prevent it.
Just remember, cancer does not depend only on good luck or bad luck. 40
It's not like a lottery. It depends on how you take care of yourself.

Five Questions Plus One

Answer the five questions. Then, make a question to be written on the blackboard for the class to answer.

① What scares most people?

② What percentage of all cancer is related to lifestyle?

③ By how much does being 40 percent overweight increase your chances of getting cancer?

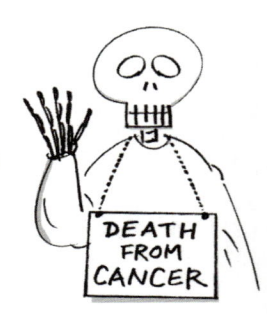

④ How much can modern medicine help cancer patients?

⑤ What does avoiding cancer mostly depend on?

Plus One

Your Question: _____

The Answer: _____

True or False Questions

Circle T (True) or F (False) for each statement. If the statement is False, rewrite it to make it True.

T F **1.** Every four minutes someone in Japan dies of cancer.

T F **2.** Whole grain (brown) rice and regular (white) rice are both high in fiber.

T F **3.** Eating ham and eggs for breakfast every day may be bad for your health.

T F **4.** Thirty percent of all cancer is caused by cigarette smoking.

T F **5.** Too much sun is bad for your skin and could eventually cause skin cancer.

Using Key Words Correctly

Write the missing word in each sentence by choosing a word from the WORD LIST below. One word is used in twice. Use your glossary if necessary.

1. A disease in which abnormal cells grow out of control and spread around the body is _____.

2. People who feel _____ think they can do nothing to prevent cancer.

3. A chemical used in the processing of meats to keep them fresh is called _____.

4. Foods made from milk, such as cheese and ice cream, are called _____ foods.

5. You should _____ dangerous food, places, and activities.

6. One meaning of _____ is to heal, make better, or become healthy.

7. To make meats like ham last longer and taste better, makers _____ them by salting or smoking.

8. If tobacco causes cancer, then we can say that tobacco is _____ to cancer.

9. A _____ is a game of chance in which you might win a prize or money—or get cancer.

10. Meat (chicken or beef) that has very little fat on it is called _____ meat.

WORD LIST		
• nitrite	• helpless	• avoid
• lottery	• dairy	• cure
• cancer	• lean	• related

Getting Information Ⓐ

Exchange information about who might get cancer by asking and answering questions like these below. Cover your partner's page.

Does Del have cancer in the family?	Yes, he does.
Is Pat overweight?	No, she isn't.

Does Bill have a stressful job?	No, he doesn't.
Does Judy like sunbathing?	Yes, she does.

Do you eat brown rice?	Yes, I do.
Do you smoke cigarettes?	No, I don't.

Are you free of stress?	Yes, I am.
	No, I'm not.

1. Practice the above sentence patterns.
2. Fill in the information for "you" in the chart below.
3. Ask the questions necessary to get the information.
4. Decide who you think is most/least likely to get cancer.

Factors:

Lifestyle	1 Smokes Tobacco	2 Is Obese	3 Eats Brown Rice	4 Eats Junk Food	5 Likes Sun-Bath-ing	6 Skips Breakfast	7 Is Free of Stress	8 Gets Good Exercise	9 Eats Lots of Vegeta-bles	10 Cancer In Family*
REIMI	yes	yes	no	yes	yes	no	no		yes	no
MITSUKO	no	no	yes	no	no		yes	yes	yes	no
HOOPY	yes	yes		yes	yes	yes	no	no	no	yes
YOU										
YOUR PARTNER										

*A non-lifestyle factor important in determining who might get cancer.

Best answers: no no yes no no no yes yes yes no

1. Who is most likely to get cancer? _____

2. Who is least likely to get cancer? _____

3. For the 10 factors listed, what is your score? _____/10

4. What must you do to get a perfect score? _____

_____   _____

Getting Information Ⓑ

Exchange information about who might get cancer by asking and answering questions like these below. Cover your partner's page.

Does Del have cancer in the family? Is Pat overweight?	Yes, he does. No, she isn't.
Does Bill have a stressful job? Does Judy like sunbathing?	No, he doesn't. Yes, she does.
Do you eat brown rice? Do you smoke cigarettes?	Yes, I do. No, I don't.
Are you free of stress?	Yes, I am. No, I'm not.

1. **Practice the above sentence patterns.**
2. **Fill in the information for "you" in the chart below.**
3. **Ask the questions necessary to get the information.**
4. **Decide who you think is most/least likely to get cancer.**

Factors:

Lifestyle	1 Smokes Tobacco	2 Is Obese	3 Eats Brown Rice	4 Eats Junk Food	5 Likes Sun-Bath-ing	6 Skips Breakfast	7 Is Free of Stress	8 Gets Good Exercise	9 Eats Lots of Vegeta-bles	10 Cancer In Family*
REIMI		yes	no	yes	yes	no	no	no	yes	no
MITSUKO	no	no	yes		no	no	yes	yes	yes	no
HOOPY	yes	yes	no	yes	yes	yes	no		no	yes
YOU										
YOUR PARTNER										

A non-lifestyle factor important in determining who might get cancer.

Best answers: no no yes no no no yes yes yes no

1. Who is most likely to get cancer? _____

2. Who is least likely to get cancer? _____

3. For the 10 factors listed, what is your score? _____/10

4. What must you do to get a perfect score? _____

_____ _____

Dialogue Dictation   06

Jeff meets his friend, Dick, whom he hasn't seen for a long time. Jeff is surprised because Dick is holding a large bag which is full of money.

Jeff: Where _____ you _____ all that _____?

Dick: From insurance. Last _____ I was _____ I had _____ and had only _____ months to _____.

Jeff: But, _____ still _____.

Dick: Of course, the _____ made a _____. I _____ have _____.

Jeff: You _____ very _____.

Dick: Yes, _____ I got _____ million _____ from my _____ insurance _____.

Jeff: So, _____ you're a _____ man.

Dick: That's right, but I'm _____ happy. I'd _____ have _____ than money.

Jeff: What _____ you _____?

Dick: Those chemotherapy* _____ made _____ my _____ fall _____!

*Key word, see Glossary p.158

⊃ **Check your answers by using the Dialogue Practice page.**

Dialogue Practice

1. Read; 2. Remember; 3. Look Up; and 4. Speak. After you finish, change roles and do it again.

A

Jeff: Where **did** you **get** all that **money**?

Dick: ....
....

Jeff: But, **you're** still **alive**.

Dick: ....
....

Jeff: You **were** very **lucky**.

Dick: ....
....

Jeff: So, **now** you're a **rich** man.

Dick: ....
....

Jeff: What **do** you **mean**?

Dick: ....
....

B

Jeff: ....

Dick: From insurance. Last **year** I was **told** I had **cancer** and had only **three** months to **live**.

Jeff: ....

Dick: Of course, the **doctor** made a **mistake**. I **didn't** have **cancer**.

Jeff: ....

Dick: Yes, **plus** I got **20** million **yen** from my **cancer** insurance **company**.

Jeff: ....

Dick: That's right, but I'm **not** happy. I'd **rather** have **hair** than money.

Jeff: ....

Dick: Those chemotherapy **treatments** made **all** my **hair** fall **out**!

You and Your Partner

The 7 Signs of Cancer: $C^1A^2U^3\ T^4I^5O^6N^7$

There are seven (7) early warning signs that can mean you have cancer. You should know them. Two out of every three people with early signs of cancer can be cured if they seek medical attention immediately.

1. **Use your glossary to find the meanings of words you don't know. Write them in the spaces at the bottom (1–12).**
2. **Answer the questions for yourself (Yes or No).**
3. **Ask your partner the questions. Write his/her answers (Yes or No).**

Do you have . . .	You	Partner
① **C**hange in toilet habits[1]?		
② **A** sore[2] that does not heal[3]?		
③ **U**nusual bleeding[4]?		
④ **T**hickness or lumps[5] on your body?		
⑤ **I**ndigestion[6]/difficulty in swallowing[7]?		
⑥ **O**bvious change in a wart[8] or mole[9]?		
⑦ **N**agging cough[10] or hoarseness[11]?		

(Note: You could have cancer and not have any pain[12]!)

Using your glossary, write the Japanese meanings of the 12 words below before you do the questions.

1. habits _____
2. sore _____
3. heal _____
4. bleeding _____
5. lump _____
6. indigestion _____

7. swallowing _____
8. wart _____
9. mole _____
10. cough _____
11. hoarseness _____
12. pain _____

 **Read This**

What Is Cancer?

Cancer is not just one disease. It is the name for many diseases in which the same thing happens: something goes wrong with the smallest living part of our bodies, the cell.

Our bodies are made up of many tiny cells. These cells together form tissue. This tissue makes up different parts of the body, for example, the skin, blood, and the brain. Cells have to make new cells to replace those that die or are damaged.

Cancer occurs when a cell becomes abnormal and starts making more abnormal cells. These abnormal cells then attack healthy cells. Sometimes the cancer cells spread to other parts of the body.

People who have cancer are normally treated by surgery, radiation, or drugs.

Choose a word(s) on the right to finish the statement.

1. Cancer is the name for many ( ).	**a.** spread
2. The smallest part of our body is a ( ).	**b.** radiation
3. Many cells together make ( ).	**c.** diseases
4. In cancer, a cell becomes ( ).	**d.** tissue
5. Sometimes cancer cells ( ).	**e.** cell
6. Cancer cells sometimes attack ( ).	**f.** abnormal
7. One treatment for cancer is ( ).	**g.** healthy cells

 **Listening for Content** 07

Read, listen, and then write to complete the sentences.

Some Bad News about Cancer

After many years of medical research there is still no general cure for cancer. In fact, the number of cancer cases has been rising in Japan—probably as the result of a more westernized lifestyle. Unfortunately, the five-year survival rate of cancer patients is only around 50 percent. Here are some reasons why:

1. Cancer often _____ to other _____ of the _____, making _____ difficult.

2. Doctors still _____ know why a _____ body _____ becomes a _____ cell.

3. Cancer has the _____ to become _____ to _____ drugs used _____ it.

4. If _____ one _____ cell _____ treatment, it can _____ and _____ later.

5. It is _____ to get _____ to _____ their _____ to _____ preventable cancer.

REMEMBER THIS
Getting cancer or not isn't just a matter
of bad luck or good luck. It mostly depends on
lifestyle—how you take care of yourself.

Activities for Conversation Practice

A Agree or Disagree

What is your opinion of the following statement? Make notes in the appropriate box and get ready to give your reasons when asked by your teacher or your partner.

It is easy to change your lifestyle to prevent cancer.

AGREE	DISAGREE

B Create a Dialogue

One student be A and the other be B. Work together and write out five exchanges of at least five words each. Practice, then do the dialogue in front of the class.

1. **A** and **B** are in a restaurant. **A** wants to give **B** a cigarette, buy him a bacon sandwich, and then go to the beach to lie in the sun. **B** thinks these are unhealthy ideas.

2. **A**'s friend, **B**, is in the hospital with cancer. **A** visits him and tries to cheer him up.

3. **A** is president of the Japan Cancer Society. **B** is president of Japan Tobacco Incorporated. They are having a discussion.

C Topics for Discussion and Writing

Individual and group. Write out your answers for the following questions, then discuss them with your classmates.

1. Stomach cancer is number one in Japan. In your opinion, why?

2. Make a list of five jobs that might have a high risk of cancer. Explain why you think they have.

3. How many words can you make out of the letters that spell C-H-E-M-O-T-H-E-R-A-P-Y? (Note: only "E" and "H" may be used twice in a word.)

🎧 08

Smoking Tobacco Is Dangerous

   It has been known for many years that tobacco smoke is dangerous—it causes sickness and death. About 80% of all lung cancers are caused by smoking. That's only lung cancer; other kinds of cancer and other diseases are also caused by tobacco smoke. Tobacco use is the number one

5 preventable cause of illness and death, and it is a world-wide problem.

   Why is tobacco smoke dangerous? The answer is simple. It is because smoke is a poisonous gas. People who die in house fires usually die from the smoke, not the flames. People who inhale tobacco smoke also die from the smoke, although much more slowly. It usually takes many

10 years before cancer develops seriously. But by the time a person finds out he has cancer, it is often too late because the three-year survival rate for lung cancer is less than 50 percent. The danger is real: one pack of cigarettes a day puts one liter of tar in a smoker's lungs in a year. Each cigarette shortens the smoker's life by eight minutes.

15   Tobacco smoke contains these poisonous substances: carbon monoxide, cyanide, tar, and nicotine. These chemicals destroy healthy body cells. Not only is smoking dangerous, it is dirty, too. It makes your mouth, hair, and clothes smell bad. It makes your teeth brown and your face look old. In addition, cigarettes can cause fires, and cigarette butts often become
20 litter and are bad for the environment wherever people smoke.

    Although the rate of smoking in Japan has been decreasing, the rate of lung cancer is still increasing. This is because of the time lag involved. Have you ever met someone who has tried to quit smoking? Most will tell you that it is very difficult. This is because smoking is more than just
25 a bad habit: it is an addiction caused by nicotine. Inhaled nicotine in the smoke travels through the blood vessels to the brain and stimulates the central nervous system, which makes the smoker feel good. When the nicotine level in the blood goes down, the smoker becomes depressed and irritable, and smokes again to feel better. Thus, the smoker is trapped in a
30 vicious circle of depression and stimulation. Sadly, this is a deadly circle.

Second-hand Smoke Is Dangerous, Too

    If you don't smoke, that does not mean that you are out of danger, because second-hand smoke is unhealthy, too. Second-hand smoke is the smoke you breathe when someone near you smokes a cigarette. For
35 example, a non-smoker married to a smoker has a greater chance of becoming ill, as do children in the family.

    Can you think of one good point of smoking cigarettes? If your answer is stress relief, you are wrong about that because smoke actually causes physical stress on the body. Some young people think smoking makes
40 them look and feel older and more mature. That is foolish, too. Any way you look at it, smoking is all minuses and no pluses.

    So, if you are wise and don't smoke, that's good; don't start. If you smoke, stop now. And, finally, avoid breathing smoky air.

Five Questions Plus One

Answer the five questions. Then, make a question to be written on the blackboard for the class to answer.

① What percentage of lung cancer is caused by smoking?

② What kind of gas is tobacco smoke?

③ Why is lung cancer increasing in Japan while smoking is decreasing?

④ What is in tobacco smoke that causes addiction?

⑤ What is second-hand smoke?

Plus One

Your Question: _____

The Answer: _____

True or False Questions

Circle T (True) or F (False) for each statement. If the statement is False, rewrite it to make it True.

T   F   **1.** Illness and death from smoking are preventable.

T   F   **2.** One pack of cigarettes a day puts a half-liter of tar in a smoker's lungs in a year.

T   F   **3.** Nicotine in the blood stimulates the central nervous system.

T   F   **4.** Non-smokers never have to worry about lung cancer.

T   F   **5.** Smoking tobacco makes you look older and more mature.

Matching for Understanding

Choose the expression on the right that means the same as the word on the left, as it is used in the text.

1. lungs ( )   **a.** to draw air/smoke into the lungs

2. disease ( )   **b.** lacking good sense or judgment

3. preventable ( )   **c.** organs inside the chest for breathing

4. poison ( )   **d.** small part remaining after smoking

5. cigarette butts ( )   **e.** well-considered action or judgment

6. litter ( )   **f.** solving a problem leads to a new one

7. rate ( )   **g.** amount or level of something

8. second-hand ( )   **h.** able to be stopped from happening

9. addiction ( )   **i.** taking air in/out of body with the lungs

10. inhale ( )   **j.** rubbish left lying around outside

11. vicious cycle ( )   **k.** something that has already been used

12. ill (illness) ( )   **l.** unable to give up using harmful things

13. breathe ( )   **m.** substance that harms or kills people

14. foolish ( )   **n.** illness caused by bacteria or other germs

15. wise ( )   **o.** being in an abnormal state of poor health

🍃 Getting Information Ⓐ

Get information about the smoking habits of four people by asking the questions below and filling in the chart. First, write in the information for yourself. Do not look at your partner's page.

How old is Katsumi?	He's/She's 48.
What is Yoriko's age?	Her/his age is 36.

Does he/she smoke?	Yes, he/she does.
Is Judith a smoker?	No, he/she isn't.

How many cigarettes does he/she smoke in a day?	He/She smokes 11 cigarettes a day.
How much does he/she smoke?	Two packs a day.

What brand does he smoke?	His brand is Lark.
What kind does she smoke?	She smokes Camel.

How long has he/she been smoking?	He's/She's been smoking for 18 years.
When did she begin smoking?	About 15 years ago.

Yoriko　　**You**　　**Partner**　　**Katsumi**

(Draw pictures of you and your partner in the space above.)

Name	Age	Smoker	Number*	Brand	Years
Katsumi	41		2 packs	Lark	
Yoriko		yes			3
Judith	48		—	—	—
You					
Partner					

Number per day

1. Who probably won't get lung cancer? _____

2. Who has the greatest chance of getting lung cancer? _____

Getting Information Ⓑ

Get information about the smoking habits of four people by asking the questions below and filling in the chart. First, write in the information for yourself. Do not look at your partner's page.

How old is Katsumi? What is Yoriko's age?	He's/She's 48. Her/his age is 36.
Does he/she smoke? Is Judith a smoker?	Yes, he/she does. No, he/she isn't.
How many cigarettes does he/she smoke in a day? How much does he/she smoke?	He/She smokes 11 cigarettes a day. Two packs a day.
What brand does he smoke? What kind does she smoke?	His brand is Lark. She smokes Camel.
How long has he/she been smoking? When did she begin smoking?	He's/She's been smoking for 18 years. About 15 years ago.

 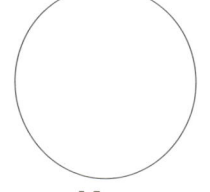  

Yoriko   *You*   *Partner*   *Katsumi*

(Draw pictures of you and your partner in the space above.)

Name	Age	Smoker	Number*	Brand	Years
Katsumi		yes			18
Yoriko	39		8	Peace	
Judith		no	—	—	—
You					
Partner					

*Number per day

1. Who probably won't get lung cancer? _____

2. Who has the greatest chance of getting lung cancer? _____

 ## *Dialogue Dictation* 09

Chris and his girlfriend, Becky, are sitting in a tea shop. Chris wants to smoke, but Becky doesn't want him to. They are arguing about this problem.

Chris: Why _____ you _____ my _____?

Becky: Because it's _____ and smells _____.

Chris: Then _____ go _____ and _____.

Becky: No. If you _____, I won't _____ you.

Chris: Why _____?

Becky: Because _____ makes _____ _____

smell _____.

Chris: This is a _____. I _____ to smoke, but I

_____ to _____ you, too.

Becky: You _____ to _____, either the _____

or _____.

Chris: Then, I'll _____ you _____ and smoke

_____.

Becky: It's too _____ to _____.

Chris: I _____ a _____ now. I _____

_____.

Becky: You are a _____. Kiss your _____ cigarette. I'm

going _____. Good-bye!

⊃ *Check your answers by using the **Dialogue Practice** page.*

Dialogue Practice

1. Read; 2. Remember; 3. Look Up; and 4. Speak. After you finish, change roles and do it again.

A

Chris: Why **don't** you **like** my **smoking**?

Becky: ....
....

Chris: Then **I'll** go **outside** and **smoke**.

Becky: ....
......

Chris: Why **not**?

Becky: ....
....

Chris: This is a **problem**. I **want** to smoke, but I **want** to **kiss** you, too.

Becky: ....
....

Chris: Then, I'll **kiss** you **now** and smoke **later**.

Becky: ....

Chris: I **need** a **cigarette** now. I **can't wait**.

Becky: ....
....

B

Chris: ....

Becky: Because it's **unhealthy** and smells **bad**.

Chris: ....

Becky: No. If you **smoke**, I won't **kiss** you.

Chris: ....

Becky: Because **smoking** makes **your breath** smell **bad**.

Chris: ....
....

Becky: You **have** to **choose**, either the **cigarette** or **me**.

Chris: ....
....

Becky: It's too **early** to **kiss**.

Chris: ....
....

Becky: You are a **fool**. Kiss your **dirty** cigarette. I'm going **home**. Good-bye!

You and Your Partner

The Bad Effects of Smoking
—16 Reasons Not to Smoke—

Study the illustration and look up any words that you don't know. Then, use the examples below to ask and answer questions.

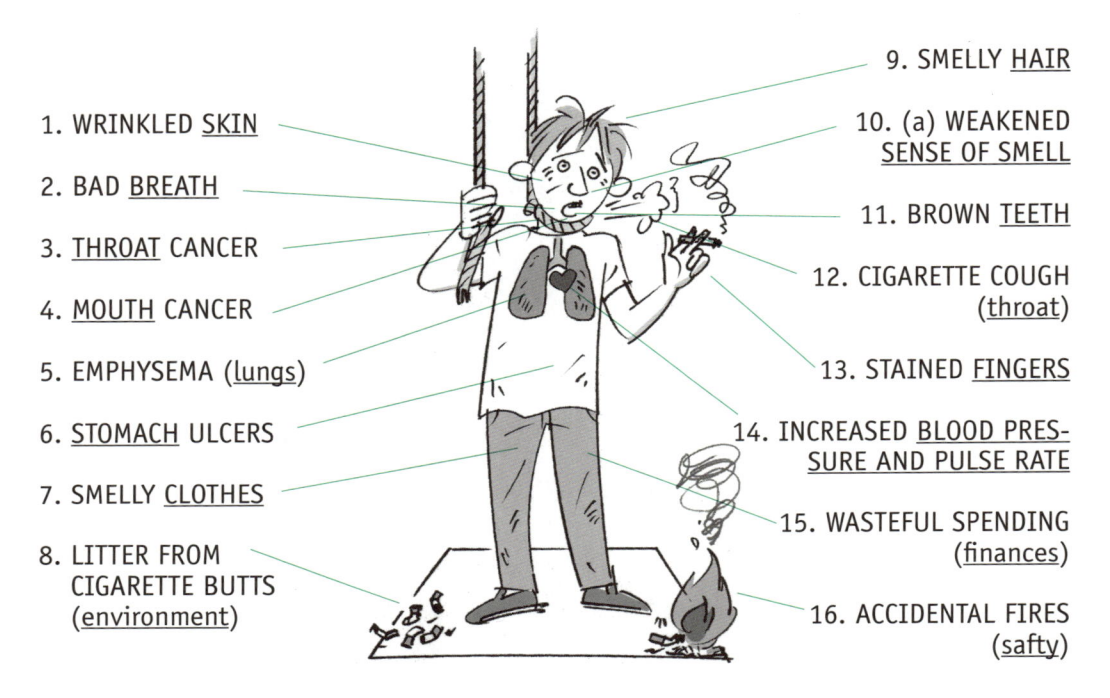

9. SMELLY <u>HAIR</u>

1. WRINKLED <u>SKIN</u>

10. (a) WEAKENED <u>SENSE OF SMELL</u>

2. BAD <u>BREATH</u>

11. BROWN <u>TEETH</u>

3. <u>THROAT</u> CANCER

12. CIGARETTE COUGH (<u>throat</u>)

4. <u>MOUTH</u> CANCER

5. EMPHYSEMA (<u>lungs</u>)

13. STAINED <u>FINGERS</u>

6. <u>STOMACH</u> ULCERS

14. INCREASED <u>BLOOD PRES-SURE AND PULSE RATE</u>

7. SMELLY <u>CLOTHES</u>

15. WASTEFUL SPENDING (<u>finances</u>)

8. LITTER FROM CIGARETTE BUTTS (<u>environment</u>)

16. ACCIDENTAL FIRES (<u>safty</u>)

Smoking often results in sickness and a slow death; however, this poor man is suffering so much he wants to make it fast!

Take turns to answer the following question, after completing the question with an <u>underlined</u> word or phrase. For example:

QUESTION

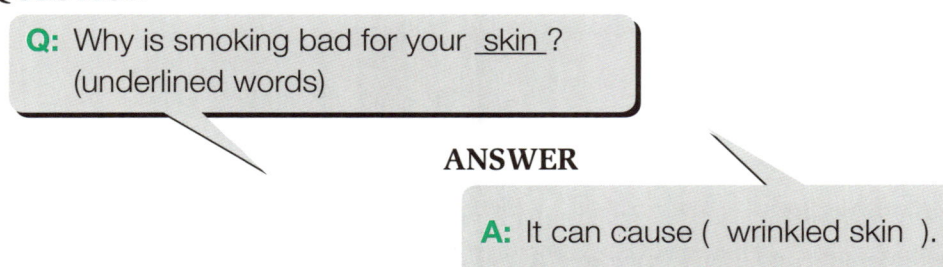

Q: Why is smoking bad for your <u>skin</u>? (underlined words)

ANSWER

A: It can cause (wrinkled skin).

When Smokers Quit

Just 20 minutes after you've smoked that last cigarette, your body begins an ongoing series of good changes:

20 MINUTES
- Blood pressure drops to normal
- Pulse rate drops to normal
- Temperature of hands and feet increases to normal

1 YEAR
- Risk of coronary heart disease is half that of a smoker

8 HOURS
- Carbon-monoxide level in blood drops to normal
- Oxygen level in blood increases to normal

1–9 MONTHS
- Coughing, nasal congestion, fatigue, shortness of breath decrease
- Cilia regrow in lungs, increasing ability to handle mucus, clean the lungs, reduce infection

24 HOURS
- Chance of heart attack decreases

2 WEEKS TO 3 MONTHS
- Circulation improves
- Lung function increases up to 30 percent

48 HOURS
- Nerve endings start regrowing
- Ability to smell and taste is enhanced
- Walking becomes easier

Q: What happens in your body _____ after quitting smoking?
(time)

A: _____

Read, listen, and then write to complete the sentences.

The Most Common Cause of Lung Cancer

Lung cancer is usually caused by carcinogens*. They can be chemicals, radiation, and some viruses. One chemical carcinogen is tar, which comes from smoking tobacco.

Key word, see Glossary p.147

1. Doctors _____ the most _____ carcinogen is

   _____, which is _____ in tobacco _____.

2. When tobacco _____ is inhaled, the _____ in the

   _____ collects in the _____.

3. There, the _____ causes _____ cell _____.

4. Eventually, the _____ of the _____ changes from

   _____ to _____.

5. In the _____, the lungs can no _____ pass

   _____ into the _____.

Activities for Conversation Practice

A Agree or Disagree

What is your opinion of the following statement? Make notes in the appropriate box and get ready to give your reasons when asked by your teacher or your partner.

> Tobacco smoke is a poison, so it should be illegal to make and sell cigarettes

AGREE	DISAGREE

B Create a Dialogue

One student be A and the other be B. Work together and write out five exchanges of at least five words each. Practice; then do the dialogue in front of the class.

1. **A** is a boys' soccer coach who smokes in front of his players. **B** is a player's mother who thinks **A** is setting a bad example for the team.

2. **A**, who is dying of lung cancer in the hospital, cannot stop smoking. He smokes secretly when no one is in the room. One day, the doctor, **B**, catches him smoking and scolds him.

C Topics for Discussion and Writing

Individual and group. Write out your answers for the following questions, then discuss them with your classmates.

1. In 1966, 84 percent of Japanese men smoked. Why do you think so many men smoked in the 1960s?

2. In Japan, the number of men smokers is decreasing, but the number of women smokers is increasing. Why do you think this is so?

3. In Japan, men smoke openly in public any time they want to. But, many women smoke only at home, or when no one is watching them. Why is this so?

🎧 00

The Environment and Your Health

The environment, which sustains life, is also a source of sickness and death for many people around the world. Although Japan is an advanced, developed country, we are also affected in harmful ways. The fertilizer- and pesticide-laced foods we eat, the dirty air we breathe, and the artificial

5 chemicals added to our food can cause harm to our bodies. On a larger scale, there is the problem of global warming from "greenhouse gases." A study in the U.S. reported that climate change over the coming years is likely to cause increased rates of allergies, asthma, heart disease, cancer, and other illnesses. It also causes extreme weather patterns such as floods,

10 droughts, and heat waves, which affect our food supply.

Let's look at some environmental problems specific to Japan. Take waste, for example: It has been reported that the amount of waste products is so great that one year's amount would make piles as high as 15 Mt. Fujis! About 50% of Japan's garbage is packaging. The disposable

15 wooden chopsticks we use every day not only add to the waste problem but also cause the loss of millions of trees (rain forests) particularly in

Southeast Asia. Noise pollution is a problem in Japan's crowded cities. Although some traffic noise is unavoidable, other noise, such as from bull horns, is preventable.

Japan relies heavily on nonrenewable sources of energy, primarily fossil-based fuels imported from far away. Oil, for example, is a major polluter, from the black exhaust fumes you see coming from a diesel bus or truck to the millions of kerosene heaters in use during the winter months. Japan's drinking water, once pure and healthy, is now so polluted and so treated with chemicals that most people have to boil their water or buy bottled water.

The ways in which our environment is under stress are too many to list here. Unfortunately, awareness of these ecological issues and problems is still low. The good news is there are many actions we can take to live "clean and green" and improve the situation. Here are just a few:

- **Waste less.** Ask stores not to overwrap your purchases. Use "doggy" bags to take home uneaten food. Use your own plastic chopsticks.
- **Recycle and Re-use.** Use your own shopping bags. Repair things instead of simply throwing them away. Use a composter in your garden.
- **Eat local food.** Choose organically-grown, as much as possible, because organic farming uses only safe, natural agricultural methods.
- **Do volunteer work.** Either on your own or through an NGO. Such simple things as picking up trash along the roads benefits nature.
- **Transportation.** Rely less on cars; use public transportation, or, better yet, walk and use bicycles as much as possible.
- **Other.** There is no end to the small things each one of us can do to protect our environment: Use energy-efficient light bulbs and appliances; use fans more and coolers less; clean air-conditioner filters regularly; buy only energy-efficient products; turn off lights and electrical appliances when not using them; follow "Warm Biz" and "Cool Biz" to keep heating and cooling energy consumption down; and so on.

It is very important that each of us increase our awareness of how to save our precious environment. Awareness, responsibility and action, plus small changes in our lifestyles, will create a healthier environment for everyone.

Five Questions Plus One

Answer the five questions. Then, make a question to be written on the blackboard for the class to answer.

① Climate change causes extreme weather patterns. Why is this bad?

② About half of Japan's garbage comes from what?

③ What source of energy does Japan rely heavily on?

④ Why is using "doggy bags" a good idea?

⑤ What four things will create a healthier environment?

Plus One

Your Question: _____

The Answer: _____

True or False Questions

Circle T (True) of F (False) for each statement. If the statement is False, correct it to make it True.

T   F   **1.** Some chemicals added to our food can cause harm to us.

T   F   **2.** Using wooden chopsticks causes the loss of thousands of trees.

T   F   **3.** It is certain that Japan's drinking water is pure and safe.

T   F   **4.** Organic farming uses only safe, natural agricultural methods.

T   F   **5.** One way people could save energy is by using fans more and coolers less.

Using Key Words Correctly

Write the missing words in the short essay below by choosing a word from the WORD LIST below. Use your glossary if necessary.

THE IMPORTANCE OF TREES

Trees are as important to humans as food and [1]_____. Trees clean the air of toxic chemicals such as carbon [2]_____ and otherpollutants. They also produce about 30% of the oxygen on [3]_____ The trees lining city streets can save up to 50% on air-conditioning in the summer and control [4]_____ pollution. Forests hold soil in place and keep water from running off the land. Trees provide shelter, food, recreation, beauty, and homes for birds, insects, and other animals. We use the [5]_____ from trees in many ways, from paper to houses.

We could not exist if there were no [6]_____. Sadly, we are destroying them faster than they can grow. Rainforests, which are vital to the earth's health, are decreasing yearly. Many birds and animals have become [7]_____ due to tree loss. Climate change has badly affected the trees which give us coffee and [8]_____ beans.

In Japan, about 60% of the [9]_____ is mountain forests; however, Japan is one of the biggest importers of wood in the world. Seventy percent of Japan's building materials come from overseas. Eighty percent of Japan's chopsticks are [10]_____. It is estimated that 20 percent of Japan's imported timber comes from illegally logged trees, mainly in Southeast [11]_____.

We need to become more aware of the threat to the world's trees and use wood resources wisely. One good thing we can do is this: [12]_____ a tree.

WORD LIST			
a. imported	d. trees	g. cocoa	j. earth
b. noise	e. water	h. Asia	k. land
c. dioxide	f. wood	i. plant	l. extinct

Getting Information Ⓐ

Choose what you think is the correct answer, then read the question to your partner. Listen to your partner's answer and check your answers.

Answer correct?

1. What is the cleanest country in Asia?
   a. Japan   **b.** Taiwan   **c.** Singapore   **d.** Hong Kong   **Yes   No**

2. How many cigarette vending machines are there in Japan?
   a. 300,000   **b.** 400,000   **c.** 500,000   **d.** 600,000   **Yes   No**

3. When is Earth Day?
   a. March 22   **b.** April 22   **c.** May 22   **d.** June 22   **Yes   No**

4. How many oil spills are there in the world every day?
   a. 7   **b.** 17   **c.** 27   **d.** 37   **Yes   No**

5. What dangerous construction material is still in many Japanese buildings?
   a. plastic   **b.** asbestos   **c.** concrete   **d.** copper   **Yes   No**

6. How many billion kilograms of trash are dumped into the oceans each year?
   a. 2 billion   **b.** 4 billion   **c.** 6 billion   **d.** 9 billion   **Yes   No**

7. About how many Japanese have died from Minamata Disease?
   a. 2-3,000   **b.** 3-4,000   **c.** 4-5,000   **d.** 5-6,000   **Yes   No**

8. What popular fish used in sushi is close to becoming extinct?
   a. snapper (tai)   **b.** salmon (sake)   **c.** bluefin tuna (toro)   **Yes   No**

9. What percent of household waste can be recycled?
   a. 50%   **b.** 65%   **c.** 72%   **d.** 84%   **Yes   No**

10. What country uses the most disposable chopsticks (waribashi)?
   a. China   **b.** Japan   **c.** Indonesia   **d.** Taiwan   **Yes   No**

Answers for your partner's questions:
1. d. 60% of Japan's shoreline is concrete.
2. d. Mongolia is the most polluted country in the world.
3. c. 3.8 million trees are cut down every year to make chopsticks
4. d. Iceland is the healthiest country in the world.
5. d. The USA uses 25% of the world's resources.
6. a. The world's honey supplies are being destroyed.
7. b. Cedar (sugi) has replaced half of Japan's natural trees.
8. c. Switzerland has the highest recycling rate.
9. c. Japan consumes 80% of the world's tuna (toro).
10. c. Fish in the oceans have decreased by 75% in recent years.

Getting Information Ⓑ

Choose what you think is the correct answer, then read the question to your partner. Listen to your partner's answer and check your answers.

Answer correct?

1. What percent of Japan's shoreline is concrete?
   a. 30%   **b.** 40%   **c.** 50%   **d.** 60%   **Yes No**

2. What is the most polluted country in the world?
   a. India   **b.** Russia   **c.** China   **d.** Mongolia   **Yes No**

3. How many trees in China are cut down to make chopsticks?
   a. 1.8 million **b.** 2.8 million **c.** 3.8 million **d.** 4.8 million   **Yes No**

4. What is the healthiest country in the world?
   a. Japan   **b.** USA   **c.** Sweden   **d.** Iceland   **Yes No**

5. What country has 5% of the world's population but uses 25% of resources?
   a. China   **b.** Russia   **c.** Indonesia   **d.** USA   **Yes No**

6. Climate change is destroying what sweet commodity?
   a. honey   **b.** cocoa   **c.** corn fructose   **d.** sugar   **Yes No**

7. Half of Japan's natural forests have been replaced with what kind of tree?
   a. pine (matsu)   **b.** cedar (sugi)   **c.** cypress (hinoki)   **Yes No**

8. What country in the world has the highest recycling rate?
   a. Germany   **b.** USA   **c.** Switzerland   **d.** Japan   **Yes No**

9. Japan consumes what percent of the world's tuna (toro)?
   a. 60%   **b.** 70%   **c.** 80%   **d.** 90%   **Yes No**

10. Fish in the oceans have decreased by how much in recent years?
    a. 35%   **b.** 55%   **c.** 75%   **d.** 85%   **Yes No**

Answers for your partner's questions:

1. c. Singapore is the cleanest country in Asia.
2. b. There are 400,000 cigarette vending machines in Japan.
3. b. Earth day is April 22.
4. c. There are 27 oil spills in the world each day.
5. b. Asbestos is still in many Japanese buildings today.
6. c. 6 billion kilograms of trash are dumped in the oceans each year.
7. a. Between 2-3,000 Japanese have died from Minamata Disease.
8. c. Blue fin tuna (toro) is close to becoming extinct.
9. d. 84% of household waste can be recycled.
10. b. Japan uses the most disposable chopsticks (waribashi).

A boy takes his girlfriend to a high-class restaurant to impress her on their first date. At the end of the meal, there is a lot of left-over food.

Boy: It looks like we _____ too _____ food.

Girl: Yes, I am on a _____ and can't _____ very much.

Boy: Do you _____ it's okay to ask for a "_____ Bag?"

Girl: Are you _____ to give that _____ food to your _____?

Boy: No, I _____ have a dog. I will eat it for _____ tomorrow.

Girl: Why? Are you a _____ man?

Boy: I have _____, but I don't want to _____ food. One-third of _____ in the world do not have enough to eat, you _____.

Girl: Wow, you are _____ a good _____. When is our _____ date?

Boy: How about lunch _____ at _____ apartment?

Girl: That _____ be great. I hope you don't _____ if I bring my big, hungry dog!

Dialogue Practice

1. Read; 2. Remember; 3. Look Up; and 4. Speak. After you finish, change roles and do it again.

A

Boy: It looks like we **ordered** too **much** food

Girl: ……………………………….. …………………………………

Boy: Do you **think** it's okay to ask for a "**Doggy** Bag?"

Girl: ………………………………… …………………………………

Boy: No, I **don't** have a dog. I will eat it for **lunch** tomorrow.

Girl: …………………………………

Boy: I have **money**, but I don't want to **waste** food. One third of **people** in the world do not have enough to eat, you **know**.

Girl: ………………………………… …………………………………

Boy: How about lunch **tomorrow** at **my** apartment?

Girl: ………………………………… ………………………………….. …………………………………

B

Boy: …………………………………. …………………………………..

Girl: Yes, I am on a **diet** and can't **eat** very much.

Boy: …………………………………. …………………………………..

Girl: Are you **going** to give that **expensive** food to your **dog**?

Boy: …………………………………. …………………………………..

Girl: Why? Are you a **poor** man?

Boy: …………………………………. ………………………………… ………………………………… …………………………………

Girl: Wow, you are **really** a good **man**. When is our **next** date?

Boy: …………………………………. …………………………………

Girl: That **would** be great. I hope you don't **mind** if I bring my big, hungry dog!

 ## You and Your Partner

 **Think Green**

MY ENVIRONMENTAL ASSESSMENT

1. I separate and recycle bottles, cans, paper, etc.
❏ Never ❏ Rarely ❏ Sometimes ❏ Often ❏ Always

2. I drink water that I know is free from chemicals and metals.
❏ Never ❏ Rarely ❏ Sometimes ❏ Often ❏ Always

3. I don't allow cigarette smoke in my apartment or near me.
❏ Never ❏ Rarely ❏ Sometimes ❏ Often ❏ Always

4. I carry my own shopping bag.
❏ Never ❏ Rarely ❏ Sometimes ❏ Often ❏ Always

5. I choose local-grown, organic food as much as possible.
❏ Never ❏ Rarely ❏ Sometimes ❏ Often ❏ Always

6. I use public transportation, bicycle, or go places on foot.
❏ Never ❏ Rarely ❏ Sometimes ❏ Often ❏ Always

7. I pick up trash when I see it on the street.
❏ Never ❏ Rarely ❏ Sometimes ❏ Often ❏ Always

8. I take home left-over food when I eat in a restaurant.
❏ Never ❏ Rarely ❏ Sometimes ❏ Often ❏ Always

9. I don't use my cooler or heater unless it is absolutely necessary.
❏ Never ❏ Rarely ❏ Sometimes ❏ Often ❏ Always

10. I volunteer my time and effort to improve the environment.
❏ Never ❏ Rarely ❏ Sometimes ❏ Often ❏ Always

Ask your partner how often he does each of these things:

Q: How often do you _____?

A: I _____ _____

 **Read This**

"Doggie Bags"

What is a Doggie Bag?
A Doggie Bag is a container used to take home left over food at restaurants. It is a good way to eliminate waste in society. The custom is most popular in the U.S.A. where it began in 1949. Today, about 90% of Americans take home food, one reason being that food portions are "super-sized," just too much to eat. The custom has spread around the world. In China, you can even take home hot soup!

Why are they called Doggie Bags?
In the beginning, people were too shy to say, "I want to take this food home." They thought others might think they were "cheap" or "poor." Nowadays, everyone knows that the food will probably be eaten by the customer, not a dog. The term is still popular, although some people say "to-go bag" or "box."

How about Doggie Bags in Japan?
A government survey found that in Tokyo alone, food accounts for 30% of all household waste. That's about 6,000 tons a day, which is enough to keep 4.5 million people alive for a day. And, Japan is a country that imports 60% of its food! The good news is that Doggie Bags are gaining popularity in Japan.

Is there anything bad about Doggie Bags?
A Doggie Bag sounds like a good idea: "Let's not waste food; let's give it to our pets." But, the Doggie Bag is a result of over-consumption—cooking, ordering, and eating too much, at a time when millions of people in the world don't have enough to eat.

Should a boy ask for a Doggie Bag on a date?
No, he should not ask for a Doggie Bag—unless he never wants to see the girl again!

QUESTIONS
How often do you use Doggie Bags? _____

What is the best kind of food to take home? _____

Have you ever felt guilty about leaving food in a restaurant?

_____

Would you ask for a Doggie Bag on a date? Why or why not?

_____

 # Listening for Content 13

Read, listen, and then write to complete the sentences.

Going Green

   Have you considered changing your lifestyle and "Going Green" for a better environment? Now is the time to change because the earth can not wait.

1. Green _____ is a _____ that helps take

   _____ of the earth.

2. You can do this by _____ only what you really _____

   of the _____ resources.

3. You should also be _____ not to _____ the

   _____ in any way.

4. It will be easier to Go _____ if you _____ that envi-

   ronment _____ your _____.

5. Environment means the _____, water, _____, chemi-

   cals, _____, and even noise.

6. Going Green is a lifestyle _____ that can make our

   _____ a better _____ to live.

Activities for Conversation Practice

A Agree or Disagree

What is your opinion of the following statement? Make notes in the appropriate box and get ready to give your reasons when asked by your teacher or your partner.

> **Drinking clean water is more important than breathing clean air.**

AGREE	DISAGREE

B Create a Dialogue

One student be A and the other be B. Work together and write out five exchanges of at least five words each. Practice; then do the dialogue in front of the class.

1. **A** is in a volunteer group that picks up trash every Sunday morning. He tries to get his friend, **B**, to join, but **B** says he wants to sleep on Sundays.

2. **A** is wondering why honey has become so expensive. **B** explains to him that climate change has damaged plants and the pollen that bees feed on.

3. **A** is playing his favorite music very loudly. **A**'s girlfriend, **B**, tells him that loud music can damage the ears and says she will go home because of it.

C Topics for Discussion and Writing

1. A Japanese survey found that Hokkaido residents are the most satisfied with their natural environment. Why do you think this is so?

2. Make a list of 5 things you need to do to live a green life.

3. What kind of renewable energy do you think is best? Why?

🎧 14

Exercise for Good Health

It is easier not to exercise. It is easier to take an elevator than it is to climb the stairs. It is easier to drive than to walk. It is easier to lie in bed than it is to jog on a cold winter morning. Unfortunately, the good things in life do not always come easily, and a healthy body is a good thing.
5 Good health requires effort—you have to work at it.

As you get older, your body condition naturally gets worse, but especially so if you are inactive. Your body is like a car engine: it will wear out or lose power much sooner if you neglect it. Unfortunately, some people take better care of their car engines than they do of their bodies,
10 even though body maintenance (exercise) is cheaper. For good body maintenance, you must exercise regularly.

These are some of the merits of regular exercise: Longer Life; Better Sleep; More Energy; Better Body Shape; Relief from Stress; Weight Loss.

Most people do know the importance of exercise, yet surveys show

that only 10 percent of adults get enough of it. If you are in the 90 percent 15
group, you must be a member of the "TOO" Club. "TOO" Club members
say they are TOO busy, TOO tired, TOO sick, TOO young, or TOO old
to exercise. Or that exercise is TOO boring. Ask yourself this: do you
have about 90 minutes of free time in your weekly schedule? It only takes
about 90 minutes a week to exercise properly. "Properly" means to choose 20
an activity such as running or swimming that will increase your heart
and lung performance to at least 70 percent of capacity over a 30-minute
period, at least three times a week. (Choosing an activity you enjoy will
help you to continue for a long time.) This would be about 2,000 calories
worth of exercise. Such exercise is called aerobic exercise. 25

Start now and set up your training schedule. Decide to do it for at least
six weeks. Why six weeks? Because most people give up after a few
weeks. In addition, after six weeks you can begin to feel the benefits.
Once you know how good exercise makes you look and feel, you will
want to make it a part of your daily life. 30

Even if you don't have time to play sports, there are many things you
can do as part of your daily life to keep in shape. Here are four things:
1. WALK, DON'T RIDE. Walking (or cycling) instead of driving for
   about 30 minutes a day is enough to keep you in good physical
   shape. 35
2. USE THE STAIRS, NOT THE ELEVATOR. The higher the stairs,
   the more this can improve heart and lung capacity.
3. DO PHYSICAL WORK. Work such as gardening or cleaning that
   requires body movement and use of muscles adds to overall fitness.
4. STRETCH YOUR BODY. You can do this anywhere, anytime. It 40
   improves blood circulation and prevents muscle stiffness.

Remember, becoming healthy takes effort; it's not easy, but it's worth it.
So, whenever you feel too lazy to exercise—but you know you should—
think about this expression: "If you don't use it, you lose it."

Five Questions Plus One

Answer the five questions. Then, make a question to be written on the blackboard for the class to answer.

① What things in life do not always come easily?

② What merits does exercise have?

③ How much time is necessary for a proper exercise program?

④ Are you a member of the "TOO" Club? Why or why not?

⑤ What do you think "If you don't use it, you lose it" means?

Plus One

Your Question: _____

The Answer: _____

True or False Questions

Circle T (True) or F (False) for each statement. If the statement is False, correct it to make it True.

T   F   **1.** It is not difficult to exercise regularly.

T   F   **2.** Most people are so busy they don't have 90 minutes of free time a week for exercising.

T   F   **3.** You should burn about 2,000 calories a week through exercise.

T   F   **4.** After a few weeks of exercising, you can feel the benefits.

Matching for Understanding

Choose the expression on the right that means the same as the word on the left, as it is used in the text.

1. merits ( )		**a.** become no good; get old
2. choose ( )		**b.** keep doing
3. capacity ( )		**c.** for walking to upper floor
4. relief ( )		**d.** not interesting
5. give up ( )		**e.** good points
6. neglect ( )		**f.** slow run
7. schedule ( )		**g.** unit of body energy
8. continue ( )		**h.** not give attention to
9. wear out ( )		**i.** unwilling to work
10. properly ( )		**j.** correctly; the right way
11. calorie ( )		**k.** select; decide upon
12. stairway ( )		**l.** helping or making better
13. boring ( )		**m.** plan or timetable
14. lazy ( )		**n.** stop; quit; drop out
15. jog ( )		**o.** full amount; 100 percent

Getting Information Ⓐ

Get information about the exercise habits of four people, including your partner. Ask the questions necessary to fill in your chart. Do not look at your partner's page.

How old is (Richard)? — He's (40) years old.
What is (Richard's) age? — His age is (37).

What kind of exercise does she/he do? — He/She (dances/swims).
He/She (plays soccer).
What's his/her exercise? — It's (walking/tennis).

How many hours a week does he/she (golf)? — He (golfs) (one hour) a week.
(Four) hours a week.
How many years has he/she been (golfing)? — He's/She's been (playing golf) for (20) years.

What's his/her physical condition like? — It's fair.   It's good.
It's poor.   It's great.
What kind of condition is he/she in? — He's/She's in (good) physical condition.

Name	Age	Exercise	*Hours	Years	Condition
Lilly		bowling		7	poor
Cally	38			2	good
Leslie	45	golf	4		
You**					
Partner					

*Hours per week
**If you don't exercise, fill in the chart with an exercise you would like to do.

1. Lilly exercises more than Cally, but she is in poorer condition. Why?

2. Among all five people in the chart, who has the best exercise program? Who has the worst? Why?

3. If your partner doesn't exercise, why not?

4. If you don't exercise, why not?

Getting Information Ⓑ

Get information about the exercise habits of four people, including your partner. Ask the questions necessary to fill in your chart. Do not look at your partner's page.

How old is (Richard)? What is (Richard's) age?	He's (40) years old. His age is (37).
What kind of exercise does she/he do? What's his/her exercise?	He/She (dances/swims). He/She (plays soccer). It's (walking/tennis).
How many hours a week does he/she (golf)? How many years has he/she been (golfing)?	He (golfs) (one hour) a week. (Four) hours a week. He's/She's been (playing golf) for (20) years.
What's his/her physical condition like? What kind of condition is he/she in?	It's fair. It's good. It's poor. It's great. He's/She's in (good) physical condition.

Name	Age	Exercise	*Hours	Years	Condition
Lilly	19		4		poor
Cally		jogging	3	2	
Leslie	45			15	fair
You**					
Partner					

*Hours per week
**If you don't exercise, fill in the chart with an exercise you would like to do.

1. Lilly exercises more than Cally, but she is in poorer condition. Why?

2. Among all five people in the chart, who has the best exercise program? Who has the worst? Why?

3. If your partner doesn't exercise, why not?

4. If you don't exercise, why not?

 **Dialogue Dictation** 15

Pete and Dick are talking in a tea room. Across the street is a sports club, and next to it is a _pachinko_ parlor.

Pete: What are _____ going to do _____, Dick?

Dick: I'm _____ to that _____ club to

_____.

Pete: Why _____ you _____?

Dick: Because _____ makes me more _____.

Pete: Is _____ why you _____ so many

_____?

Dick: Yes, _____ _____.

Pete: I _____ every _____, but I _____ find a

_____.

Dick: Where _____ you _____?

Pete: In that _____ over _____.

Dick: The _____ club?

Pete: No, next _____ it, the _____ place.

Dick: What _____ of _____ can _____ do in

a _pachinko_ _____?

Pete: It's _____ "_____" exercise.

Dick: Are _____ _____? Healthy _____ won't

_____ you find a _____!

⊃ _Check your answers by using_
  the **Dialogue Practice** _page._

Dialogue Practice

1. Read; 2. Remember; 3. Look Up; and 4. Speak. After you finish, change roles and do it again.

A

Pete: What are **you** going to do **today**, Dick?

Dick: ....

Pete: Why **do** you **exercise**?

Dick: ....

Pete: Is **that** why you **have** so many **girlfriends**?

Dick: ....

Pete: I **exercise** every **day**, but I **can't** find a **girlfriend**.

Dick: ....

Pete: In that **building** over **there**.

Dick: ....

Pete: No, next **to** it, the *pachinko* place.

Dick: ....

Pete: It's **called** "**finger**" exercise.

Dick: ....

B

Pete: ....

Dick: I'm **going** to that **sports** club to **exercise**.

Pete: ....

Dick: Because **exercise** makes me more **handsome**.

Pete: ....

Dick: Yes, **it is**.

Pete: ....

Dick: Where **do** you **exercise**?

Pete: ....

Dick: The **sports** club?

Pete: ....

Dick: What **kind** of **exercise** can **you** do in a *pachinko* **parlor**?

Pete: ....

Dick: Are **you crazy**? Healthy **fingers** won't **help** you find a **girlfriend**!

You and Your Partner

My Exercise Schedule

Plan an exercise program for three days a week. Write the information in the chart below, then answer your partner's questions about it.

Exercise	Days	Start Time	Finish Time	Hours	Place

Sample Questions/Answers:

Q. What exercise are you going to do?
A. I'm going to (swim/jog/play tennis/ski/ etc.).

Q. On what days are you going to (swim/jog/play tennis/ski/ etc.)?
A. I'm going to _____ on _____, _____, and _____.

Q. For how long are you going to _____?
A. I'm going to _____ for _____ hours.

Q. Where are you going to _____?
A. I'm going to _____ at/in _____.

My Partner's Exercise Schedule

Exercise	Days	Start Time	Finish Time	Hours	Place

Who do you think has the best program from an aerobic point of view?

I think *I have/My partner has* the best one because _____ _____.

 **Read This**

The Aerobics System

Aerobic exercises are exercises based on science that improve heart and lung efficiency. The system was made famous by Dr. Kenneth Cooper of the U.S.A.

Using the aerobics point system in the charts below, answer the questions.

CHART 1
FITNESS LEVELS
(Points per Week)

Fitness	Men	Women
Very Poor	00–09	00–07
Poor	10–20	08–15
Fair	21–31	16–26
Good	32–50	27–40
Excellent	51–74	41–64
Superior	75+	65+

CHART 2
WALKING/JOGGING PROGRAM

Activity	Distance	Time	One Week	=	Points
Walking	3.0 km	32 min	3 times		13.5
Walking	5.0 km	48 min	3 times		21.7
Walk/Jog	3.0 km	26 min	4 times		24.9
Walk/Jog	3.0 km	24 min	4 times		28.0
Jogging	3.0 km	22 min	4 times		31.6
Jogging	3.0 km	20 min	4 times		36.0
Jogging	4.0 km	25 min	4 times		46.0
Jogging	4.0 km	23 min	4 times		49.5
Jogging	5.0 km	30 min	4 times		56.0
Jogging	5.0 km	27 min	4 times		61.3

1. For a man to get a "good" level of fitness, how many points a week are necessary? For a woman?

2. If a woman jogger gets only 16 points a week, what would her fitness level be? In the case of a man?

3. If a woman jogs five km in 27 minutes four times a week, how many points would that be? What level? In the case of a man?

4. If you began a walking/jogging program today, how many points do you think you could get? Why?

Read, listen, and then write to complete the sentences.

How to Exercise Safely

Exercise can be dangerous if you are not careful. Some people have had heart attacks while jogging, for example. Here are six rules to help you exercise safely:

1. Get a _____ checkup before _____ an

   _____ program.

2. Warm _____ for about _____ minutes before

   _____ to exercise.

3. Start _____ and _____ the _____ of

   exercise _____.

4. Know _____ body's _____ and don't _____

   .

5. Exercise _____, but _____ when you _____

   feeling _____.

6. Always _____ down _____ exercising by

   _____ moving _____.

Activities for Conversation Practice

A Agree or Disagree

What is your opinion of the following statement? Make notes in the appropriate box and get ready to give your reasons when asked by your teacher or your partner.

> **Japanese company workers doing exercise before work is a waste of time.**

AGREE	DISAGREE

B Create a Dialogue

One student be A and the other be B. Work together and write out five exchanges of at least five words each. Practice; then do the dialogue in front of the class.

1. **A** is an American who just started working for a Japanese company. He cannot understand the custom of group exercises every morning. He asks **B**, a Japanese colleague, to explain the custom.

2. **A** is 78 years old, but he hopes to run in the New York Marathon. **B**, his grandson, is worried and asks him a lot of questions about his condition.

C Topics for Discussion and Writing

Individual and group. Write out your answers for the following questions, then discuss them with your classmates.

1. In Japan, experts say the physical condition of children is getting worse every year. What do you think is the reason for this?

2. Most trainers, including Dr. K. Cooper, say that cross-country skiing is the best aerobic exercise. Why would this be?

3. In recent years, Japan has become weaker in international sports competition. In your opinion, why is this happening?

🎧 17

Healthy Food for a Healthy Body

"You are what you eat" is often said by nutrition experts. It means that your diet (what you eat) is the foundation for your physical and emotional well-being. Would you want to cross bridges or be in buildings without good foundations? Of course not! But, many of us have bodies with poor
5 foundations because of unhealthy eating habits.

Once again, think of your body as an engine, and think of food as fuel—for humans. When your engine is getting good fuel and running smoothly, you're healthy, energetic, and physically attractive. When it's getting poor-quality fuel, you're likely to be unhealthy, not energetic, and
10 overweight. To prevent that from happening, think about nutrition and eat wisely. Develop a positive eating plan by knowing which foods are good for you and which aren't. Then form good eating habits and don't change. This is not easy to do because there is so much delicious food around us all the time, and eating is one of life's great pleasures. Unfor-

tunately, although they sound alike, "delicious" doesn't always equal 15 "nutritious." Actually, much of the food people love—like potato chips, candy, ice cream, and cola—is not healthy. That means these foods are not good fuel for your body.

These so-called "junk foods," dished out in fast-food restaurants, supermarkets, and convenience stores, have increased considerably in 20 recent years. This reflects the change in Japanese lifestyles with more women working and more people eating "on-the-run." The convenience and standardized tastes of such foods may be an advantage because they save time. However, there is a "price to pay" in nutrition because they contain more sugar, salt, and artificial seasonings than home-cooked 25 food. In addition, they are treated with food additives for color, flavor, and preservation. No one really knows the long-term effects all these chemicals have on the human body.

An average person needs about 2,500 calories a day from complex carbohydrates, protein, and fats. A balanced variety of natural foods from 30 the four basic food groups below should give you all the vitamins and minerals you need: (1) milk products; (2) meat, fish, chicken, and eggs; (3) vegetables and fruits; and (4) bread and rice.

Some points to remember are these: Eat a lot of fresh fruits, vegetables, and high-fiber foods. Cut down on the meat and high-cholesterol 35 foods. Drink pure, nutritious drinks like milk and juice, not coffee and sodas. Reduce or eliminate the use of salt and sugar; they are in most food already.

If you had lived in Japan many years ago, choosing good food would have been simple. People had little choice then; they had to eat what they 40 could get, which was the traditional, fresh-grown, vegetable-based diet. Today, we have more than enough food, but much of it is unnecessary or unhealthy. This food is one cause of health problems like heart disease, diabetes, stomach cancer, and obesity.

Think about your diet. Remember, "You are what you eat." This simply 45 means that eating good food makes you healthy, happy, and—really— even handsome.

Five Questions Plus One

Answer the five questions. Then, make a question to be written on the blackboard for the class to answer.

① What does "You are what you eat" mean?

② Why is it difficult to follow a good diet?

③ What are the four basic food groups?

④ What was the traditional Japanese diet like?

⑤ What health problems are caused by unhealthy eating?

Plus One

Your Question: _____

The Answer: _____

True or False Questions

Circle T (True) or F (False) for each statement. If the statement is False, correct it to make it True.

T   F   **1.** Food can be thought of as a kind of fuel.

T   F   **2.** All delicious food is good for your health.

T   F   **3.** To "cut down" on a food means to eat less of it.

T   F   **4.** People who lived 100 years ago probably were not fat.

T   F   **5.** Most food doesn't have enough sugar or salt in it.

Using Key Words Correctly

Write the missing word in each sentence by choosing a word from the WORD LIST below. Use your glossary for words you don't understand.

1. The science of food and how it affects your health is called

   _____.

2. _____ food is good for your health because it contains many

   nutrients.

3. Being _____ may be one result of poor eating habits.

4. Something you do regularly is called a _____.

5. Food can taste _____ but not be nutritious.

6. To _____ a food from your diet means to stop eating it.

7. A _____ diet means a variety of food from each food group.

8. Eating too many foods high in _____ could cause heart

   disease.

9. The _____ Japanese diet has always been a healthy diet.

10. The scientific name for being fat is _____.

11. Good food is a kind of _____ for the body.

12. A person who is _____ has a lot of energy.

WORD LIST		
• overweight	• balanced	• cholesterol
• nutritious	• foundation	• nutrition
• traditional	• habit	• obesity
• eliminate	• energetic	• delicious

Getting Information Ⓐ

Answer these questions about your eating habits. Then, use the sample sentences to ask your partner questions about his/her eating habits. A plus (+) or a minus (–) indicates good or bad from a nutritional point of view. Cover your partner's page.

How often do you . . . Do you ever . . .		You				Partner			
		always	often	some-times	never	always	often	some-times	never
miss lunch?	–								
eat brown bread?	+								
drink green tea?	+								
eat brown rice?	+								
drink cola?	–								
eat fresh fruit?	+								
eat *natto*?	+								
go to Lotteria?	–								
*									

Your original question

| always | often | sometimes | never |

Question How often do you / Do you ever   miss breakfast? / eat fast food?

Answer I | always / often / sometimes / never   eat fast food. / do. / miss breakfast.

Getting Information (B)

Answer these questions about your eating habits. Then, use the sample sentences to ask your partner questions about his/her eating habits. A plus (+) or a minus (–) indicates good or bad from a nutritional point of view. Cover your partner's page.

How often do you . . . Do you ever . . .		You				Partner			
		always	often	some-times	never	always	often	some-times	never
miss lunch?	–								
eat brown bread?	+								
drink green tea?	+								
eat brown rice?	+								
drink cola?	–								
eat fresh fruit?	+								
eat *natto*?	+								
go to Lotteria?	–								
*									

*Your original question

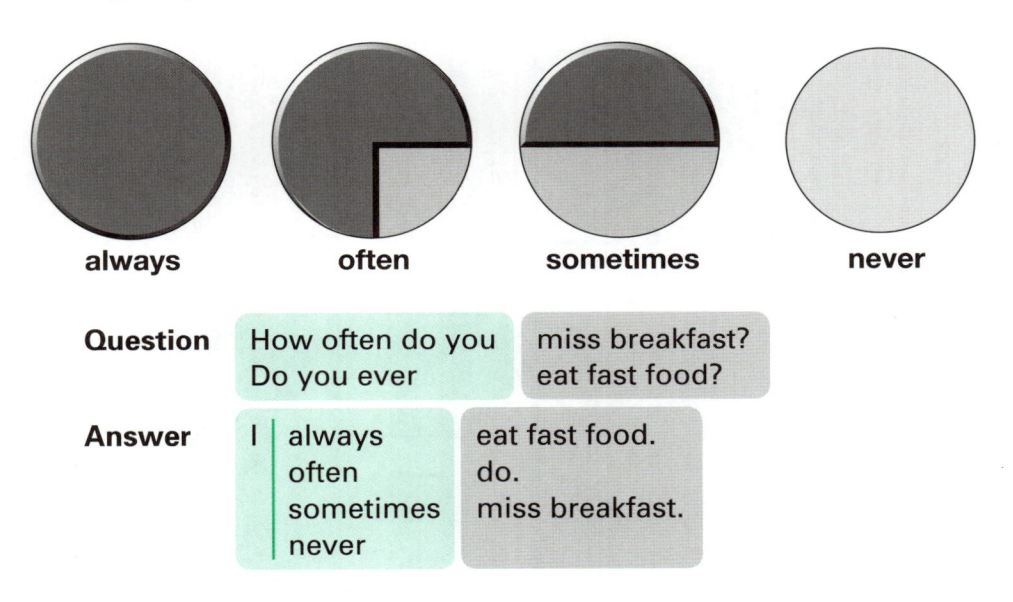

| always | often | sometimes | never |

Question	How often do you Do you ever	miss breakfast? eat fast food?
Answer	I always often sometimes never	eat fast food. do. miss breakfast.

Dialogue Dictation

18

Jim is shopping in a health food store for the first time. His friend, Liz, is giving him advice.

Jim: My ____________ food is ____________ cream. Is it ____________?

Liz: No, it's ____________ very ____________.

Jim: Why? It's ____________ from ____________, isn't it?

Liz: A ____________ milk, but mostly ____________ chemicals and ____________ of ____________.

Jim: Is there any ____________ ice ____________?

Liz: Here is some ____________ ____________ ice cream.

Jim: *Natto* ____________ cream? That sounds ____________!

Liz: But, it's ____________ in ____________.

Jim: Never ____________, I ____________ my ____________ ice cream at ____________, anyway.

Liz: What ____________ do you ____________?

Jim: ____________ ice cream.

Liz: What! Now I ____________ why you ____________ a red ____________ after ____________ ice cream.

➲ *Check your answers by using the* **Dialogue Practice** *page.*

Dialogue Practice

1. Read; 2. Remember; 3. Look Up; and 4. Speak. After you finish, change roles and do it again.

Natto ♥

A

Jim: My **favorite** food is **ice** cream. Is it **healthy**?

Liz: ....

Jim: Why? It's **made** from **milk**, isn't it?

Liz: ....

Jim: Is there any **healthy** ice **cream**?

Liz: ....

Jim: *Natto* **ice** cream? That sounds **bad**!

Liz: ....

Jim: Never **mind**, I **make** my **own** ice cream at **home**, anyway.

Liz: ....

Jim: **Alcohol** ice cream.

Liz: ....

B

Jim: ....

Liz: No, it's **not** very **healthy**.

Jim: ....

Liz: A **little** milk, but mostly **artificial** chemicals and **lots** of **sugar**.

Jim: ....

Liz: Here is some **special** *natto* ice cream.

Jim: ....

Liz: But, it's **high** in **protein**.

Jim: ....

Liz: What **kind** do you **make**?

Jim: ....

Liz: What! Now I **know** why you **get** a red **face** after **eating** ice cream.

You and Your Partner

Opinion Questionnaire

Below are some statements about food and drinks. Do you agree or disagree with them? Write your opinions, then get and write your partner's. The student answering should close his/her book. Follow this example:

All "junk food" should have warning labels on it.

[I agree.]━━━━━━[I disagree.]━━━━━━[I don't know.]

Y=You / **P**=Your Partner	AGREE		DISAGREE		DON'T KNOW	
	Y	**P**	**Y**	**P**	**Y**	**P**
① Food from a can is just as healthy as fresh food.						
② Most imported food is too dangerous to eat.						
③ Eating seaweed can make hair grow on your head.						
④ Eating carrots makes your eyesight better.						
⑤ Eggs are dangerous because of their high cholesterol.						
⑥ The legal drinking age should be raised to 22.						
⑦ Rice wine with raw eggs is a good medicine for colds.						
⑧ _Write your original statement here._						

Explain why you agree or disagree for each item.

I agree/disagree because _____.

Read This

The Importance of Water

Water is the most important substance for all living things. You can live for weeks without food, but you can only live a few days without water. It's simply precious. Remember these important facts about water:

1. Your body is about 65 percent water. For example, if you weigh 60 kilograms, about 40 kilograms is water.
   a. Your blood is 90 percent water.
   b. Your brain is 75 percent water.
   c. There is water in every body cell.
2. Water carries food (nutrients) to all cells in the body.
3. It keeps your body at the right temperature.
4. It carries wastes away through the urine.
5. You lose about two liters of water every day.
6. Water is easy to replace; it is in all food.

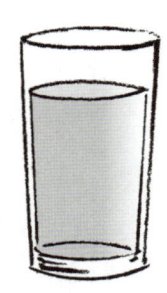

6 – 8 a day

You should drink <u>six</u> to <u>eight</u> glasses of liquids daily. Getting your liquids only in soft drinks, coffee, tea, or beer is not good. While they all contain water, the sugar, caffeine and alcohol in them can upset the fluid balance in your body—and they might make you fat.

Just plain water is best, and it's free!

How well can you remember? <u>Cover</u> the top half of this page, <u>listen</u> to the teacher's questions, and <u>write</u> your answers below.

1. _____
2. _____
3. _____
4. _____
5. _____

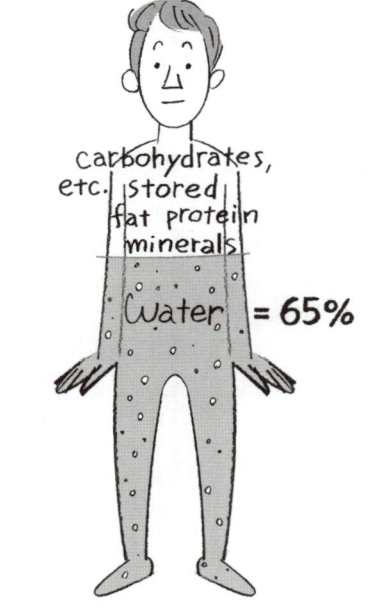

carbohydrates, etc. stored fat protein minerals

Water = 65%

Read, listen, and then write to complete the sentences.

A Guide to Proper Food Intake

For most people, the main meal of the day is eaten in the evening. However, this is not good for health. Here is a rule—called the 25-50-25 rule—that can remind you when to eat the proper amounts of food:

1. Your _____ needs _____ for _____ during

   the _____.

2. But, _____ body doesn't _____ many calories at

   _____.

3. Therefore, you should:

   a. Get _____ percent of _____ calories at

   _____.

   b. Then, another _____ percent at _____ time.

   c. But, _____ only _____ percent of your

   _____ at _____ time.

4. It is not _____ to eat _____ at _____

   before _____ to _____.

```
┌────────── 25% ────── 50%
│ Breakfast
│ Lunch
│ Dinner
│ The 25-50-25 Rule
```

Activities for Conversation Practice

A Agree or Disagree

What is your opinion of the following statement? Make notes in the appropriate box and get ready to give your reasons when asked by your teacher or your partner.

> **People should eat the food they like to eat.**

AGREE	DISAGREE

B Create a Dialogue

One student be A and the other be B. Work together and write out five exchanges of at least five words each. Practice; then do the dialogue in front of the class.

1. **A** is trying to get his young son, **B**, to drink milk for breakfast, but **B** wants to drink only coke.

2. **A** eats all his meals at fast-food restaurants. **B** is explaining why he shouldn't eat there so much.

3. **A** gets up late every morning, so he doesn't eat breakfast. His mother, **B**, is telling him how important breakfast is.

C Topics for Discussion and Writing

Individual and group. Write out your answers for the following questions, then discuss them with your classmates.

1. In the U.S. there is a jingle that goes like this: "I'm Popeye the sailor man, I'm strong to the finish 'cause I eat my spinach, I'm Popeye the sailor man." Explain what you think this jingle means.

2. Discuss your eating habits. What are the good points of your eating habits? The bad points? How do you think you can improve your diet?

3. Brown rice is more nutritious than white rice. Explain why. Do you like brown rice? Why or why not?

 20

Alcohol Can Be Dangerous

Alcohol is an old drug, and it is drunk in every part of the world. Why is alcohol so popular? Is it good for you or not? What are alcoholism and drunkenness?

Alcohol relaxes most people and helps them forget about their worries.
5 This is why it is so popular. Can you imagine a *bonenkai* without alcoholic drinks? It would be as dull as a business meeting, and no one would talk. For Japanese businessmen, after-work drinking with colleagues provides stress relief and allows for smooth communication.

Fortunately, small amounts of alcohol are usually not harmful to healthy
10 people. Some studies have even reported that a little alcohol every day, such as the custom of *banshaku*, might be good for health.

Drinking alcohol may have some good points, but basically it is not good. The two problems that may result from drinking are alcoholism and drunkenness.

Alcoholism is a serious illness. The alcoholic person loses control 15 of his drinking, and this has a harmful effect on his work, family, and health. Heavy drinkers often develop liver trouble, high blood pressure, and obesity. Beer makes you fat: gram-for-gram, it has twice as many calories as chocolate.

For most people, drunkenness is a bigger health risk than alcoholism. 20 This is because you might get drunk and be in a car accident. Drunkenness is a temporary loss of control over your reactions and behavior. Have you noticed how quickly a drinker's face gets red? Alcohol quickly goes to the brain through the blood. It slows down those parts of the brain that control judgment, thought, and muscular coordination. Alcohol affects 25 each person differently depending on these factors: your age (the legal drinking age is 20); how fast you drink; whether you have eaten; the type of drink; your body weight; and your drinking experience.

Eating before drinking can slow down alcohol's bad effects. Coffee doesn't help, although it might keep you from falling asleep. If you drink 30 too much, "time" is the only cure; it takes about 18 hours for the liver to burn up alcohol in the blood.

Drinking alcohol used to be a man's pastime, but nowadays drinking among young women has become popular. Women who drink should stop during pregnancy. Alcohol in the woman's body can cause fetal alcohol 35 syndrome, which often leads to mental retardation in the baby.

A way of drinking called "chugging" or "bottoms up" is traditionally popular among students. Known as *ikkinomi* in Japan, it is very dangerous. Rapid drinking can cause sudden death from "alcohol shock" because the body cannot cope with the abnormal rate at which alcohol is taken into 40 the blood stream. Don't do it, and don't force others to do it.

Alcohol is a drug that you don't need. Although it may ease tension, it often causes abnormal behavior. And, if you're driving, abnormal behavior could be deadly. For many people, one drink may affect driving ability.

Remember, drinking and driving do not mix! 45

Five Questions Plus One

Answer the five questions. Then, make a question to be written on the blackboard for the class to answer.

① Why is alcohol so popular?

② What happens when a person becomes an alcoholic?

③ What three physical problems can drinking cause?

④ What is drunkenness?

⑤ What two things do not go together?

Plus One

Your Question: _____

The Answer: _____

True or False Questions

Circle T (True) or F (False) for each statement. If the statement is False, correct it to make it True.

T F **1.** Chocolate has more calories than beer.

T F **2.** It takes about 18 hours for the body to rid itself of alcohol in the blood.

T F **3.** Coffee can stop you from becoming drunk.

T F **4.** Everyone needs alcohol to relieve stress and ease tension.

T F **5.** Alcohol can cause some people to do dangerous things.

Matching for Understanding

Choose the expression on the right that means the same as the word on the left, as it is used in the text.

1. temporary ( )		**a.** reduce; make less
2. ease ( )		**b.** addiction to alcohol
3. abnormal ( )		**c.** sickness
4. risk ( )		**d.** decision
5. illness ( )		**e.** being overweight
6. mix ( )		**f.** not interesting
7. coordination ( )		**g.** possibility of danger
8. dull ( )		**h.** parts moving together
9. judgment ( )		**i.** dangerous to the body
10. cause ( )		**j.** reason for something
11. alcoholism ( )		**k.** for a short time
12. harmful ( )		**l.** put together
13. obesity ( )		**m.** response to an action
14. cure ( )		**n.** not normal
15. reaction ( )		**o.** make healthy or normal

Getting Information Ⓐ

Get information about the drinking habits of four people, including your partner. Practice these patterns first: Do not look at your partner's page.

What does Masa drink?	He drinks wine.
What does Kazuyo like?	She likes *sake*.
How does Gus drink whiskey?	On the rocks.
What type of beer does Bob drink?	Dry beer.
	He drinks light.
How much does Kazu drink?	One can a day.
Where do you usually drink?	In Miyakomachi.

Answer for "You," then ask the questions and fill in the rest of the chart below. (If you don't or can't drink alcohol, list any drink.)

Name	Drink	Type	Amount*	Place
Masa	beer		3 cans	
Pete		Scotch		S. Club
Shirley	wine		5 bottles	
You				
Partner				

*Amount in one week

1. Who might become an alcoholic? _____

2. Who spends the least money on drinks? _____

3. Whose favorite drink is made from grapes? _____

4. Whose drink is the healthiest? _____

   Why? _____

✎ *Getting Information* Ⓑ

Get information about the drinking habits of four people, including your partner. Practice these patterns first: Do not look at your partner's page.

What does Masa drink?	He drinks wine.
What does Kazuyo like?	She likes *sake*.
How does Gus drink whiskey?	On the rocks.
What type of beer does Bob drink?	Dry beer.
	He drinks light.
How much does Kazu drink?	One can a day.
Where do you usually drink?	In Miyakomachi.

Answer for "You," then ask the questions and fill in the rest of the chart below. (If you don't or can't drink alcohol, list any drink.)

Name	Drink	Type	Amount*	Place
Masa		light		Bar 101
Pete	whiskey		2 bottles	
Shirley		red		at home
You				
Partner				

Amount in one week

1. Who might become an alcoholic? _____

2. Who spends the least money on drinks? _____

3. Whose favorite drink is made from grapes? _____

4. Whose drink is the healthiest? _____

   Why? _____

 **Dialogue Dictation** 21

Jon and Sue meet in a liquor store, which is a store selling alcoholic drinks. Jon is buying beer.

Sue: Jon, I _____ you _____ drinking _____.

Jon: That's _____. I _____.

Sue: Then _____ are you _____ this _____?

Jon: Because _____ is non-_____ beer.

Sue: What _____ you _____?

Jon: Well, it _____ and _____ like beer, but _____ has no _____.

Sue: That's _____! A _____ with no alcohol.

Jon: Yes, it's _____ to get _____, and your _____ doesn't become _____.

Sue: I _____ to _____ some, too.

Jon: There is one _____, though.

Sue: What _____ the _____?

Jon: It _____ a _____ party.

⊃ *Check your answers by using the* **Dialogue Practice** *page.*

Dialogue Practice

1. Read; 2. Remember; 3. Look Up; and 4. Speak. After you finish, change roles and do it again.

A

Sue: Jon, I **heard** you **stopped** drinking **alcohol**.

Jon: ....

Sue: Then **why** are you **buying** this **beer**?

Jon: ....

Sue: What **do** you **mean**?

Jon: ....

Sue: That's **amazing**! A **beer** with no alcohol.

Jon: ....

Sue: I **want** to **buy** some, too.

Jon: ....

Sue: What **is** the **problem**?

Jon: ....

B

Sue: ....

Jon: That's **right**. I **stopped**.

Sue: ....

Jon: Because **this** is non-**alcohol** beer.

Sue: ....

Jon: Well, it **looks** and **tastes** like beer, but **it** has no **alcohol**.

Sue: ....

Jon: Yes, it's **impossible** to get **drunk**, and your **face** doesn't become **red**.

Sue: ....

Jon: There is one **problem**, though.

Sue: ....

Jon: It **makes** a **dull** party.

You and Your Partner

Drinking and Driving

This chart shows how various amounts of alcohol in the blood usually affect driving ability.

355 ml beer *or* 118 ml wine *or* 36 ml whiskey

Drinks in a Two-hour Period

Weight

45	1	2	3	4	5	6	7	8	9	10	11	12
55	1	2	3	4	5	6	7	8	9	10	11	12
65	1	2	3	4	5	6	7	8	9	10	11	12
75	1	2	3	4	5	6	7	8	9	10	11	12
85	1	2	3	4	5	6	7	8	9	10	11	12

Dangerous to Drive   **Very Dangerous**   **Impossible to Drive Safely**

A. Questions

1. If a person who weighs 65 kilograms has four drinks in two hours, what will his/her driving condition be?
2. How many drinks in a two-hour period make it impossible to drive safely at any weight?

B. The exact effect of alcohol on driving ability depends on these factors: health, drinking habits, and amount, kind, and timing of food eaten.

Fill in the chart below. Write the information for yourself, then ask your partner and write his/her answers. (Questions No. 3–5 are for students over 20 years old.)

	You	Partner
① How old are you?		
② How is your health?		
③ Are you a fast or slow drinker?		
④ How long have you been drinking?		
⑤ Do you usually eat before drinking?		

Read This

The Bad Effects of Alcohol

BRAIN
Brain cells are changed and many die. Memory is slowed, and the senses are dulled.

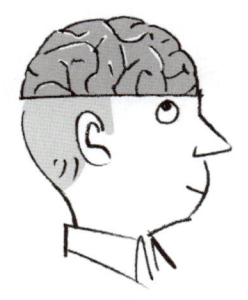

CEREBELLUM
Physical coordination is slowed.

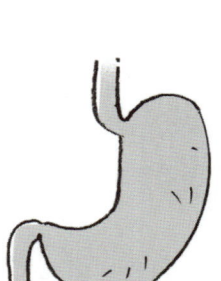

STOMACH & INTESTINES
Alcohol can cause bleeding and may cause cancer.

HEART
The heart muscle becomes weak and cannot pump blood properly.

LIVER
Alcohol damages the liver most. Eventually liver cells die from cirrhosis.

Question: What bad affect does alcohol have on the _____?

Answer: _____

Listening for Content 🎧 22

Read, listen, and then write to complete the sentences.

Some Interesting Facts about Alcohol

Here are some interesting—but little-known—facts as regards alcohol. Young people who try to get drunk in a hurry should remember fact number 6.

1. Alcohol is a _____ because it _____ calories.

2. Beer and _____ are more _____ than _____
.

3. Alcohol _____ the _____ to _____ up _____ vitamins.

4. Mixing _____ won't _____ you _____ than not _____ them.

5. When your _____ is _____, you get _____ faster.

6. A _____ can _____ from _____ too _____ too _____.

**Seatbelts save lives.
Don't drink and drive.**

Activities for Conversation Practice

A Agree or Disagree

What is your opinion of the following statement? Make notes in the appropriate box and get ready to give your reasons when asked by your teacher or your partner.

Heavy drinking is less harmful to health than heavy smoking.

AGREE	DISAGREE

B Create a Dialogue

One student be A and the other be B. Work together and write out five exchanges of at least five words each. Practice; then do the dialogue in front of the class.

1. **A**, who is drunk, is leaving a party to drive home. **B**, his friend, is trying to stop him from driving.

2. **A** is trying to get his girlfriend, **B**, to drink wine because he thinks it will make her more romantic. However, she's worried about getting fat.

3. While driving a car, **A** threw a beer can out of the window. The can hit a jogger, **B**, on the head. They are arguing.

C Topics for Discussion and Writing

Individual and group. Write out your answers for the following questions, then discuss them with your classmates.

1. Do you know anyone who is a heavy drinker? Why do you think that person drinks so much?

2. Japanese men often go to bars after work, but American men drink at home with their families. What do you think about these differences?

3. Which do you think is worse, being a heavy drinker or being a heavy smoker? Explain why.

 23

Stress Can Ruin Your Health

Japan has become a technological and economic power on the strength of its "human resources." This is good news for the Japanese people. The bad news is that this rapid progress has caused a lot of stress in society.

Japan—fast-paced, crowded, and noisy—is considered to be one of the
5 most stressful societies in the world. Consider these facts: (1) Workers work more and children study more than in most other countries; (2) Wives and mothers have to manage the home alone even though half of them have jobs; (3) Business and personal problems cause over 20,000 suicides every year; (4) In a recent survey, more than 70 percent of male
10 salaried workers feel they are overworked, and 40 percent feel they are likely to become victims of *karoshi*, death as a result of stress caused by overworking and the fear of losing their jobs.

Take the case of Ken Ono of Tokyo who worked for a large trading company. Every day, he had to spend over an hour pushing through

crowds on the train and streets to get to work. At the office, he was under 15
great pressure until 9 at night. Then, he had to go to bars and drink with
colleagues or customers until midnight. He had to play "company" golf
on Sundays. He couldn't relax at home because his expensive apartment
was too small for his wife and two noisy young children. One morning
he woke up with pains in his stomach, so he stayed home for a few days. 20
When he went back to his office, his boss said he was lazy and told him
to work harder. A week later he was in a mental hospital, a victim of
Japan's "workaholic" culture.

Everyone has stress, and a small amount of it is normal. A little stress
at times can be good, such as the stress you feel before running a race. 25
The amount of everyday stress each person experiences varies depending
on personality and lifestyle. Severe stress may result in hair loss, ulcers,
mental sickness, or heart attack. Here are five ways to fight stress:

1. SLOW DOWN.
   Live your life one step at a time at a comfortable pace. 30
2. WORRY LESS.
   Worrying about things you can't change is a waste of energy.
   Life is not perfect and we all have problems, most of which are
   smaller than we think. How you react to them is the key. Keeping
   a positive attitude will help you overcome them. 35
3. LEARN TO RELAX.
   Refresh your mind and body by exercising, playing games, or
   taking a nap. Set aside some quiet time for yourself every day.
   Laughing a lot helps, too.
4. WATCH YOUR DIET. 40
   Keep your weight down, limit salt and sugar, eat breakfast.
5. AVOID DANGEROUS CHEMICALS.
   Don't use harmful drugs like nicotine (tobacco), caffeine (coffee),
   and alcohol. You may think these drugs help you relax, but they
   produce bodily stress. 45

Don't let stress ruin your health. Start now and control it—before it
controls you!

Five Questions Plus One

Answer the five questions. Then, make a question to be written on the blackboard for the class to answer.

① What is one of the biggest problems in Japanese society?

② About how many people kill themselves every year?

③ What are some bad effects of severe stress?

④ Why shouldn't you worry about things you can't change?

⑤ What are three chemicals you should be careful about using?

Plus One

Your Question: _____

The Answer: _____

Matching for Understanding

Choose the expression on the right that means the same as the word on the left, as it is used in the text.

1. lazy ( )	**a.** short sleep in daytime
2. nap ( )	**b.** take care of
3. rapid ( )	**c.** a sore in the stomach
4. colleague ( )	**d.** not use
5. ruin ( )	**e.** disliking work
6. pain ( )	**f.** use needlessly
7. manage ( )	**g.** damage or destroy
8. waste ( )	**h.** something that hurts
9. avoid ( )	**i.** person with the same job
10. ulcer ( )	**j.** quick; fast

Finish the Sentence

Choose the best answer to finish each sentence below.

1. Stress may ruin (   ).
   a. your family life
   b. your health
   c. both a and b

2. Many wives and mothers have stress because (   ).
   a. they have two jobs
   b. they have too much free time
   c. they have too many children

3. A small amount of stress is (   ).
   a. dangerous
   b. normal
   c. not good

4. Stress can be (   ).
   a. controlled
   b. good
   c. both a and b

5. The best time to control stress is (   ).
   a. when it gets heavy
   b. all the time
   c. after drinking

6. An example of good stress would be the stress you feel when (   ).
   a. running a race
   b. your car hits a dog
   c. your father shouts at you

7. People think nicotine, caffeine, and alcohol help to relax. Actually, they are (   ).
   a. just like sleeping pills
   b. a cause of stress in the body
   c. good for quick energy

Getting Information Ⓐ

Stress and personality are related. Do the personality quiz for yourself, then ask your partner and write his/her answers, too. Use your glossary if necessary. Cover your partner's page.

What Kind of Person Are You?

Example: Q: Are you (honest)?

A: • Yes, I'm (very/a little) (honest).

• No. I'm not (honest).

Note: *Before you ask or answer questions, look up the words you don't know in the glossary.*

	Your Answers				Your Partner's Answers		
Are you?	**Not**	**A Little**	**Very**		**Not**	**A Little**	**Very**
shy							
kind							
lonely							
romantic							
selfish							
talkative							
ambitious							
emotional							
patient							
cooperative							

⬆ Your Word

Now, ask your partner "Why?" for some of the words. For example:

Q: Why are you <u>lonely/not lonely</u>?

A: Because I <u>don't have/have</u> a girlfriend.

🍃 Getting Information Ⓑ

Stress and personality are related. Do the personality quiz for yourself, then ask your partner and write his/her answers, too. Use your glossary if necessary. Cover your partner's page.

What Kind of Person Are You?

Example: Q: Are you (honest)?

A: • Yes, I'm (very/a little) (honest).

• No. I'm not (honest).

Note: *Before you ask or answer questions, look up the words you don't know in the glossary.*

Your Answers

Are you?	Not	A Little	Very
shy			
kind			
lonely			
romantic			
selfish			
talkative			
ambitious			
emotional			
patient			
cooperative			

Your Partner's Answers

Not	A Little	Very

⬆ Your Word

Now, ask your partner "Why?" for some of the words. For example:

Q: Why are you <u>lonely/not lonely</u>?

A: Because I <u>don't have/have</u> a girlfriend.

Dialogue Dictation 🎧 24

Mr. and Mrs. Joseph Watkins are suffering from stress. He feels stress because he has a high-pressure job and no time to relax. She feels stress because she works full-time and takes care of the house and family.

Mrs.: I'm tired of _____, _____, and taking

_____ of the _____.

Mr.: I _____ try to _____ you _____.

Mrs.: You use this _____ like a _____.

Mr.: I will _____ to come _____ earlier.

Mrs.: Your _____ don't _____ you.

Mr.: I _____ try to _____ with them.

Mrs.: You _____ hug _____ or _____ me.

Mr.: I will _____ you _____.

Mrs.: You _____ give me _____.

Mr.: I'll _____ you _____ you want.

Mrs.: Then I want _____.

Mr.: Do you _____ you _____ to go outside?

Mrs.: No, I want _____ of this _____!

_____. Divorce!

⊃ *Check your answers by using*
the **Dialogue Practice** *page.*

Dialogue Practice

1. Read; 2, Remember; 3. Look Up; and 4. Speak. After you finish, change roles and do it again.

A

Mrs.: I'm tired of **cooking**, **cleaning**, and taking **care** of the **children**.

Mr.: ....

Mrs.: You use this **house** like a **hotel**.

Mr.: ....

Mrs.: Your **children** don't **know** you.

Mr.: ....

Mrs.: You **never** hug **me** or **kiss** me.

Mr.: ....

Mrs.: You **never** give me **anything**.

Mr.: ....

Mrs.: Then I want **out**.

Mr.: ....
....

Mrs.: No, I want **out** of this **marriage**! **D-I-V-O-R-C-E**. Divorce!

B

Mrs.: ....
....

Mr.: I **will** try to **help** you **more**.

Mrs.: ....

Mr.: I will **try** to come **home** earlier.

Mrs.: ....

Mr.: I **will** try to **play** with them.

Mrs.: ....

Mr.: I will **love** you **more**.

Mrs.: ....

Mr.: I'll **give** you **whatever** you want.

Mrs.: ....

Mr.: Do you **mean** you **want** to go outside?

Mrs.: ....
....

 # You and Your Partner

Person of My Dreams

What points are important to you in choosing your future husband or wife?

Number each quality (A–L) from 1 to 12, with 1 being the MOST important, and 12 being the LEAST important.

Future Husband

(   ) Is intelligent   **A**
(   ) Laughs easily   **B**
(   ) Is well-educated   **C**
(   ) Has a good job   **D**
(   ) Typical Japanese   **E**
(   ) From a rich family   **F**
(   ) Is understanding   **G**
(   ) Is an only child   **H**
(   ) Is quite handsome   **I**
(   ) Same hobbies as me   **J**
(   ) Is taller than me   **K**
(   ) Is older than me   **L**

Future Wife

(   ) Is very feminine
(   ) Has a cute smile
(   ) Good personality
(   ) Traditional type
(   ) Very modern type
(   ) Likes children
(   ) Loves me a lot
(   ) Likes what I like
(   ) Is beautiful
(   ) From a nice family
(   ) Is shorter than me
(   ) Is younger than me

First, write your answers to the five questions below. Next, ask your partner and write his or her answers.

What point is . . .

	You	Partner
① the most important to you?		
② the least important to you?		
③ important to your parents?		
④ your strongest point?		

What point not listed is important to you? _____

to your partner? _____

Ask your partner to explain "Why?" for each answer.

Read This

The Bad Effects of Stress

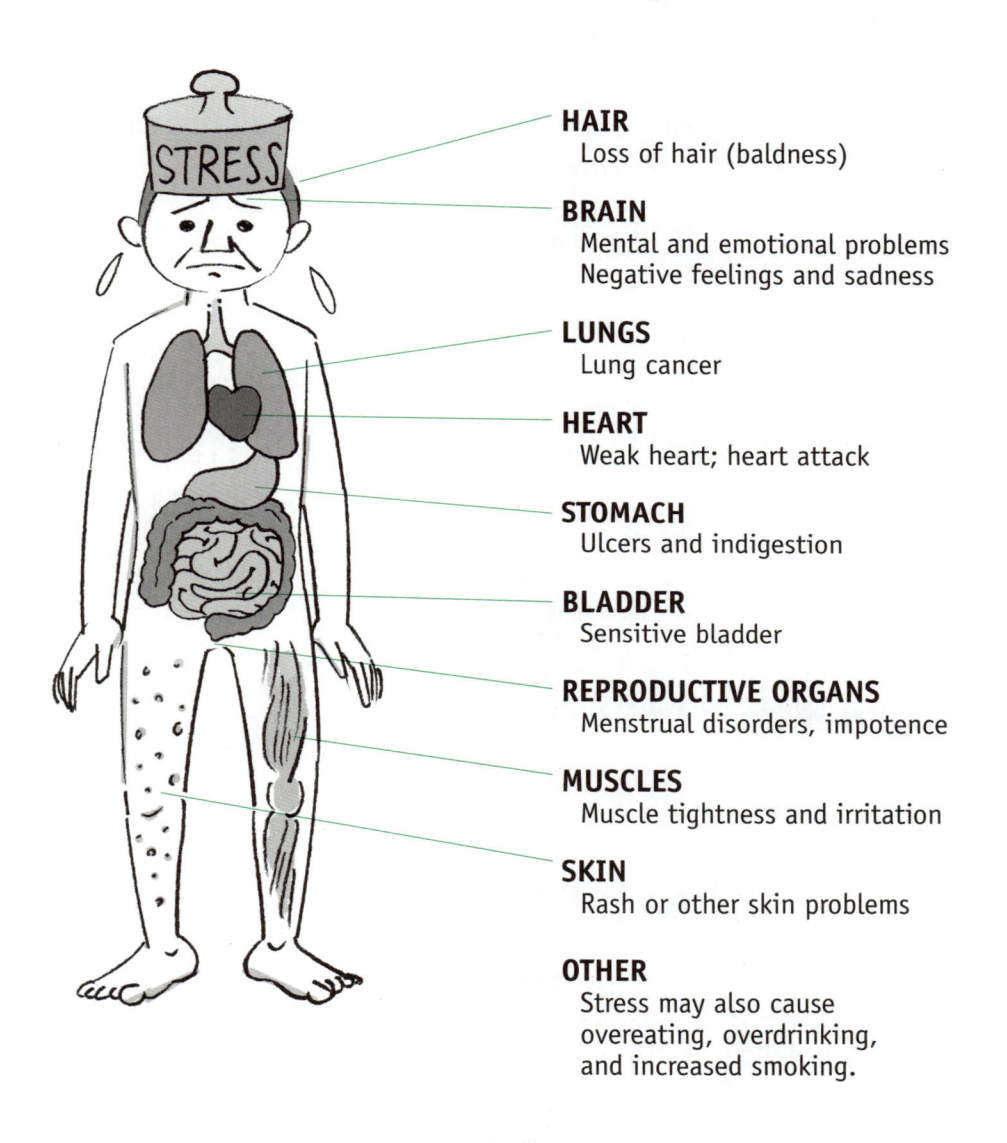

HAIR
Loss of hair (baldness)

BRAIN
Mental and emotional problems
Negative feelings and sadness

LUNGS
Lung cancer

HEART
Weak heart; heart attack

STOMACH
Ulcers and indigestion

BLADDER
Sensitive bladder

REPRODUCTIVE ORGANS
Menstrual disorders, impotence

MUSCLES
Muscle tightness and irritation

SKIN
Rash or other skin problems

OTHER
Stress may also cause
overeating, overdrinking,
and increased smoking.

You can fight stress by a change in lifestyle and positive thinking.

Q: What can stress do to your_____?

A: It can cause_____.

Q: What other things many stress cause?

A: It may cause _____, _____, and _____.

Listening for Content 🎧 25

Read, listen, and then write to complete the sentences.

Laughter for Stress Relief

Laughter is one of the best "medicines" for stress, say doctors who have studied the problem. Here is why:

1. When _____ laugh, _____ activity _____.

2. This _____ relaxing _____ to be _____ in the _____.

3. Also, _____ causes _____ to become _____ tense.

4. Therefore, _____ rate and _____ pressure _____.

5. These _____ in the _____ make you feel _____.

Activities for Conversation Practice

A Agree or Disagree

What is your opinion of the following statement? Make notes in the appropriate box and get ready to give your reasons when asked by your teacher or your partner.

> **A doctor has a more stressful job than an airline pilot.**

AGREE	DISAGREE

B Create a Dialogue

One student be A and the other be B. Work together and write out five exchanges of at least five words each. Practice; then do the dialogue in front of the class.

1. **A** thinks men have more stress in life than women. **B**, a woman, does not agree.
2. **A**'s hair is falling out, so he visits a doctor to get help. The doctor, **B**, questions him about his lifestyle.
3. **A** loves to smoke and drink, but he has just learned that he has an ulcer. The doctor, **B**, tells him that he must stop both immediately.

C Topics for Discussion and Writing

Individual and group. Write out your answers for the following questions, then discuss them with your classmates.

1. Psychologists say the three most stressful things in life are (1) death of husband or wife; (2) divorce; and (3) being put in prison. What do you think about this?
2. What kind of stress do you have in your life?
3. It is often said that, compared to Americans, Japanese do not know how to enjoy their free time. Why do you think this is a problem for Japanese?

🎧 26

Obesity Is a Bad Thing

Obesity is increasing at an alarming rate throughout the world. Today, it is estimated that there are more than 300 million obese people worldwide.

You are considered to be obese if you are at least 20 percent over your ideal weight. The Japan Obesity Association defines obesity as a Body
5 Mass Index* of 26.4 or higher. Do you know your BMI? You don't have to look like a sumo wrestler to be overweight. You could be obese and not know it!

Many years ago, obesity was not a big problem in Japan because there were no candy bars, ice cream, and "Big Macs" then, and people were
10 more physically active. Nowadays, it is a problem. Due to the increase in the amount and variety of food available—along with advertising—it is difficult to diet and stay slim. In today's lifestyle, most people sit all day at work, then sit at home in front of the TV at night, often while snacking on potato chips and drinking cola.

---

*BMI = weight ÷ [height]² × 10.000

Some people say, "I'm going to eat what I want; I don't care if I get 15
a little fat." But, getting a little fat is not the problem: the problem is,
obesity kills. It is a fact that overweight people die younger than slim
people. Also, they have more health problems such as kidney disease,
diabetes, and coronary heart trouble.

The physical cause of obesity is well-known: more calories (energy) 20
are taken in than are burned. Simply speaking, people eat more than they
need. Why people overeat is difficult to answer. Whatever the reason,
lack of self-control is usually part of the problem.

One country with a big obesity problem is the U.S.A. About 60 percent of adult Americans are overweight, which is more than double the 25
percentage of overweight Japanese. The main reason is the difference in
diet: Americans eat an average of 3,700 calories a day, while Japanese
eat an average of only 2,810. The fat content of American food is much
higher than that of Japanese food. However, both the number of calories
and amount of fat in Japanese food have been increasing greatly. 30

Often, Japanese who visit the U.S. are surprised at how many fat people
there are. They should not be surprised—Japanese are becoming fat, too.
Japan's food has become "westernized," and sweets and processed foods
are now popular. Meat consumption is going up while rice consumption
is going down. Recently, a Japanese obesity specialist said, "20 years ago 35
Japan had very little severe obesity like that seen in the United States;
now it is more common, and it's causing health problems, even among
children."

The cure for obesity is simple: reduce the amount of calorie intake, and
exercise. For quite a few people, obesity is a mental problem, a matter 40
of willpower. The key to eating well-balanced, low-calorie meals and
exercising is willpower.

You may ask, "How do I get the willpower?" The answer is, it comes
from desire—the desire to be slim and attractive, and have a long, healthy
life. 45

Five Questions Plus One

Answer the five questions. Then, make a question to be written on the blackboard for the class to answer.

① Why wasn't obesity a problem many years ago?

② Is it difficult or easy to stay slim nowadays?

③ Who die earlier, overweight people or slim people?

④ What is the physical cause of obesity?

⑤ Has the fat content of Japanese food been increasing or decreasing?

Plus One

Your Question: _____

The Answer: _____

True or False Questions

Circle T (True) or F (False) for each statement. If the statement is False, correct it to make it True.

T F **1.** Obesity can cause diabetes.

T F **2.** Americans take in more calories a day than Japanese.

T F **3.** The Japanese diet is not changing.

T F **4.** Both less calorie intake and more exercise are important in losing weight.

T F **5.** Self-control helps people stay slim.

Using Key Words Correctly

Write the missing word in each sentence by choosing a word from the WORD LIST below.

1. Your _____ weight means the weight that is best for your sex, age, and body type.

2. A _____ person is overweight (obese).

3. It is a fact that obesity _____.

4. People who overeat and become fat often lack _____.

5. The fuel or energy value of food is measured in _____.

6. To _____ calories means to physically use calories.

7. To _____ means to eat low-calorie foods. A country's _____ means what the people eat.

8. _____ foods are foods that have been changed from their natural condition.

9. _____ means the amount of something that is eaten or used.

10. The _____ send out urine (wastes) from the body.

11. Willpower often comes from a _____.

12. If you have a lot of _____, you can do difficult things.

WORD LIST		
• desire	• diet	• willpower
• consumption	• kills	• fat
• processed	• burn	• calories
• self-control	• ideal	• kidneys

Getting Information Ⓐ

Get information about your partner's weight and eating habits. Write his/her answers in the boxes. Do not look at your partner's page.

What food do you eat most often?

_____

_____

_____

_____

What is your weight?

_____

_____

_____

_____

Do you think you are overweight?

_____

_____

_____

_____

What is your favorite drink?

_____

_____

_____

_____

Would you mind having a girl/boyfriend who is fat?

_____

_____

_____

_____

What kind of candy do you like best?

_____

_____

_____

_____

Get an explanation from your partner by asking follow-up questions such as "Why?" or "Why not?"

Getting Information B

Get information about your partner's weight and eating habits. Write his/her answers in the boxes. Do not look at your partner's page.

How much do you weigh?

_____

_____

_____

_____

What is your favorite food?

_____

_____

_____

_____

How often do you check your weight?

_____

_____

_____

_____

What is your biggest meal of the day?

_____

_____

_____

_____

Have you ever been on a diet?

_____

_____

_____

_____

Do you have a lot of will-power?

_____

_____

_____

_____

Get an explanation from your partner by asking follow-up questions such as "Why?" or "Why not?"

Dialogue Dictation 27

Ichiro wants to marry. He recently had his first date with a girl introduced to him by a matchmaker (*nakodo*). The couple went to a McDonald's restaurant.

Nakodo: How ＿＿＿＿＿ your ＿＿＿＿＿ date, Ichiro?

Ichiro: It was both ＿＿＿＿＿ and ＿＿＿＿＿.

Nakodo: Why ＿＿＿＿＿ it ＿＿＿＿＿?

Ichiro: Well, the ＿＿＿＿＿ you ＿＿＿＿＿ me ＿＿＿＿＿ only her ＿＿＿＿＿.

Nakodo: Didn't ＿＿＿＿＿ have a ＿＿＿＿＿ face?

Ichiro: Yes, she ＿＿＿＿＿, but she was ＿＿＿＿＿ like a ＿＿＿＿＿-＿＿＿＿＿.

Nakodo: I see. And ＿＿＿＿＿ was it ＿＿＿＿＿?

Ichiro: At ＿＿＿＿＿, she ate ＿＿＿＿＿ "Big Macs," ＿＿＿＿＿ shakes, and ＿＿＿＿＿ apple pies!

Nakodo: So, have you ＿＿＿＿＿ not to marry her?

Ichiro: Yes. She's too ＿＿＿＿＿ and ＿＿＿＿＿ for me.

Nakodo: You had better ＿＿＿＿＿ about it ＿＿＿＿＿.

Ichiro: Why ＿＿＿＿＿ I?

Nakodo: Because she's a ＿＿＿＿＿ and ＿＿＿＿＿ profes-sional lady ＿＿＿＿＿!

↺ *Check your answers by using the Dialogue Practice page.*

Dialogue Practice

1. Read; 2. Remember; 3. Look Up; and 4. Speak. After you finish, change roles and do it again.

A

Nakodo: How **was** your **first** date, Ichiro?

Ichiro: ....
....

Nakodo: Why **was** it **surprising**?

Ichiro: ....
....

Nakodo: Didn't **she** have a **pretty** face?

Ichiro: ....
....

Nakodo: I see. And **why** was it **expensive**?

Ichiro: ....
....
....

Nakodo: So, have you **decided** not to marry her?

Ichiro: ....
....

Nakodo: You had better **think** about it **again**.

Ichiro: ....

Nakodo: Because she's a **rich** and **famous** professional lady **wrestler**!

B

Nakodo: ....
....

Ichiro: It was both **surprising** and **expensive**.

Nakodo: ....

Ichiro: Well, the **picture** you **gave** me **showed** only her **face**.

Nakodo: ....

Ichiro: Yes, she **did**, but she was **shaped** like a **body-builder**.

Nakodo: ....
....

Ichiro: At **McDonald's**, she ate **four** "Big Macs," **three** shakes, and **five** apple pies!

Nakodo: ....
....

Ichiro: Yes. She's too **big** and **strong** for me.

Nakodo: ....
....

Ichiro: Why **should** I?

Nakodo: ....
....

You and Your Partner

Your Ideal Weight

If you're a young person, you may think you don't have to worry about getting fat. But, you do. Your weight has a tendency to increase every year because you become less active, and your body becomes less efficient at using energy (calories).

Ask and answer the questions about your and your partner's weight.
H = Height; M = Male; F = Female

Ideal Weights

H	M	F
150	52.0	51.0
151	52.6	51.4
152	53.3	51.9
153	53.9	52.3
154	54.6	52.8
155	55.2	53.2
156	55.9	53.7
157	56.6	54.2
158	57.2	54.7
159	57.9	55.2
160	58.6	55.7
161	59.3	56.2
162	60.0	56.8
163	60.7	57.3
164	61.4	57.9
165	62.1	58.6
166	62.8	59.2
167	63.6	59.9
168	64.3	60.5
169	65.0	61.3
170	65.8	62.0
171	66.5	62.8
172	67.3	63.6
173	68.1	64.4
174	68.9	65.3
175	69.7	66.2
176	70.5	67.1
177	71.3	68.1
178	72.1	69.1
179	72.9	70.1
180	73.8	71.2
181	74.6	–
182	75.5	–
183	76.3	–

Q. How tall are you?
A. I am _____ centimeters tall.

Q. What is your height?
A. My height is _____ centimeters.

Q. How much do you weigh?
A. I weigh _____.

Q. What is your weight?
A. My weight is _____ kilograms.

You

1. My height is _____.
2. My weight is _____.
3. My ideal weight is _____.
4. I am _____ kilograms overweight/ underweight. (circle one)

Your Partner

1. His/Her height is _____.
2. His/Her weight is _____.
3. His/Her ideal weight is _____.
4. He/She is _____ kilograms over- weight/underweight. (circle one)

Read This

Too Skinny is Bad, Too!

With so many people overweight these days, it is easy to forget about people who are too thin.

Skinny, thin, slim, slender, underweight. All these words mean about the same. Except, however, if someone is underweight, they are too thin, and therefore not healthy. If your BMI is below 18.5, you are <u>underweight</u>.

Here is the complete BMI* scale:

```
18.5 or less  = underweight
18.5 to <25   = normal weight
25 to   <30   = overweight
30 to   <35   = obese
*BMI=weight÷[height]²×10,000
```

Being underweight can be caused by stress, medical conditions, or eating disorders such as anorexia. Anorexia is an illness in which a person has a strong fear of becoming fat, refuses to eat enough, and becomes thinner and thinner. It sometimes results in death.

How to Gain Weight:

Putting on weight sounds like it might be fun because you can eat as much ice cream, candy, and potato chips as you like, right? Wrong! Although you need more calories in your diet to gain weight, they should be good calories, not bad calories. Choose foods that are prepared with cooking methods like baking, poaching, and stir-frying. Your meals should be balanced with the right amounts of protein, carbohydrates and fat. Resistance training exercises, like weight lifting, may help to increase your muscle size, which will increase your body weight. If you are having trouble gaining weight, you might consider taking protein or weight-gaining supplements. Remember: Too skinny is bad, too!

My BMI is _____; therefore, I am _____.

Read, listen, and then write to complete the sentences.

The Snacking Habits of Americans

The custom of snacking between meals, which is called *oyatsu* in Japanese, is very popular with Americans. Too much snacking on high-calorie foods can cause obesity, however. Here are some U.S.A. "Snack Facts."

1. The most popular snacks in America are _____, potato chips, _____, cake, _____, ice cream, and

   _____.

2. Sixty-_____ percent of all Americans _____ once a

   _____ or _____.

3. Thirty-six _____ of _____ snack after _____

   .

4. The _____ person eats _____ kilograms of

   _____ per _____.

5. People over age _____ do _____ snacking than

   _____ people and _____.

Activities for Conversation Practice

A Agree or Disagree

What is your opinion of the following statement? Make notes in the appropriate box and get ready to give your reasons when asked by your teacher or your partner.

> It is easier for a slim person to find a good job than for a fat person.

AGREE	DISAGREE

B Create a Dialogue

One student be A and the other be B. Work together and write out five exchanges of at least five words each. Practice; then do the dialogue in front of the class.

1. **A**, who weighs 178 kilograms, is buying an airline ticket. **B**, the airline clerk, tells **A** he must buy two tickets (seats) because of his size. **A** disagrees.

2. **A** is angry at his wife because she has become fat. She, **B**, is angry at him because he smokes.

3. **A**, who is 140 kilograms, has an *omiai* with a girl who weighs 40 kilograms. They are discussing marriage.

C Topics for Discussion and Writing

Individual and group. Write out your answers for the following questions, then discuss them with your classmates.

1. Some people say that one reason Americans are bigger than Japanese is that food is much cheaper in the U.S.A. What do you think the reasons are?

2. The heaviest person in the world weighs over 400 kilograms. What kind of problems do you think this person has in everyday life?

3. Tell about the heaviest person you have ever met.

 29

Dental Care for Healthy Teeth

Question: what is the hardest part of your body? Answer: your teeth. Think of all the hard things you sometimes chew such as nuts and hard candy—with no damage to your teeth. Whether you chew soft or hard food, good, strong teeth are necessary. You can easily live without hair
5 on your head, but life without teeth would be difficult.

Another question: what is an often neglected part of your body? Answer: your teeth. A lot of people worry more about their hair or their makeup than they do about their teeth. Teeth are easy to take care of, but most people don't pay as much attention to them as they should. That is why
10 there are tooth decay, gum disease and dentists with scary drills.

People in remote areas of the world who have simple, natural diets have almost no tooth decay. In the modern world, with our sugar-in-everything diet, there is much tooth decay. This is how it happens: a sticky substance called plaque develops on the teeth when bacteria combine

with tiny particles of food. It develops quickly, and it contains harmful 15
acids which destroy the teeth's outer surface, the enamel. This results
in cavities. When plaque is not removed, a hard substance called tartar
collects, and this leads to gum disease, which is the cause of tooth loss
in 70 percent of adults.

The two ways to keep your teeth healthy are proper cleaning and nu- 20
trition. Follow these rules for good cleaning:

1. BRUSH YOUR TEETH AFTER EACH MEAL.
   Don't forget to brush your tongue, too.
2. USE A SOFT BRUSH AND A FLUORIDE TOOTHPASTE.
   Fluoride helps stop cavities by making tooth enamel stronger. 25
3. USE DENTAL FLOSS EVERY DAY.
   Dental floss is a nylon string that removes plaque from between
   the teeth.
4. GO TO THE DENTIST EVERY YEAR FOR A CHECKUP.

Nutrition is important, too. Your teeth especially need calcium to stay 30
strong. Good sources of calcium are milk products, fish, and eggs. What
your teeth don't need is sugar. Most snack foods are high in sugar, so be
careful about eating them. Brush your teeth after snacking if possible.

Oral cancer, or cancer of the mouth, is something you should know
about. The primary risk factors are smoking and heavy alcohol consump- 35
tion. In Japan—where men smoke and drink more than women—oral
cancer has been rising steadily among men. Symptoms to look for include: (1) a sore that bleeds easily and does not heal; (2) color change in
the mouth tissue; (3) a lump, pain, or rough spot; (4) any other abnormal
change in the mouth. Regular visits to the dentist can increase the chances 40
of early detection.

Prevention is the key. Start taking good care of your teeth now. And
don't forget to smile. A nice smile—with pretty teeth—brightens everyone's day.

Five Questions Plus One

Answer the five questions. Then, make a question to be written on the blackboard for the class to answer.

① What is the hardest part of your body?

② What is an often neglected part of your body?

③ What does plaque contain?

④ How does fluoride help stop cavities?

⑤ How often should you use dental floss?

Plus One

Your Question: _____

The Answer: _____

True or False Questions

Circle T (True) or F (False) for each statement. If the statement is False, correct it to make it True.

T   F   **1.** When adults lose their teeth, gum disease is the cause in 70 percent of all cases.

T   F   **2.** Dental floss is a nylon string that removes plaque from between the teeth.

T   F   **3.** The worst thing for your teeth is sugar.

T   F   **4.** Smoking will not make your teeth brown.

T   F   **5.** Prevention (keeping something bad from happening) is the key to healthy teeth.

Matching for Understanding

Choose the expression on the right that means the same as the word on the left, as it is used in the text.

1. chew ( )
2. neglect ( )
3. decay ( )
4. gums ( )
5. sticky ( )
6. bacteria ( )
7. particle ( )
8. enamel ( )
9. cavity ( )
10. tartar ( )
11. detection ( )
12. prevent ( )
13. proper ( )
14. tiny ( )
15. substance ( )

a. stop something from happening
b. covers outer surface of teeth
c. very small
d. something hard, it collects on teeth
e. like glue
f. crush or bite with teeth
g. correct; the right way
h. very small piece of something
i. thing you can feel or see
j. not take care of
k. a hole in a tooth
l. become rotten or no good
m. noticing or discovering something
n. small organisms (medical word)
o. part of mouth above/below teeth

Dr. Tom's Soft Brush

Getting Information Ⓐ

Exchange information about two dentists with your partner by asking and answering the questions below. Write the information you get in the two blank spaces. When you finish, check the information by looking at page 123. Cover your partner's page.

HAACK DENTAL CLINIC

_____

_____

_____

_____

_____

_____

_____

PULLUM DENTAL PLAZA

❑ Dr. I. Pullum, D.D.S.
❑ 317-2 Morrison Road
❑ Tel. 12-3525 or 19-3712
❑ In Basement of Central Hotel, Room 339
❑ Hours: 9–9, Every Day
❑ No Appointment Necessary
❑ Free Checkup for Young Children (Under 6)

CHILDREN'S DENTISTRY

❑ Dr. Makum Screem, D.D.S.
❑ Tel. (078) 139-9399
❑ 5661 Bruce Crossing Road (One Block West of Station)
❑ Appointment Required
❑ Children Only to Age 13
❑ Fluoride Treatment Given
❑ Free Parking Available
❑ Play Room for Children

WEDRILL TEETH CARE

_____

_____

_____

_____

_____

_____

_____

_____

Questions:

1. What is the name of the dentist?
2. How do you spell that?
3. What is the telephone number?
4. What is the address?
5. Where, exactly, is it?
6. How do I get there?
7. Is an appointment necessary?
8. What are the hours?
9. What is their speciality?
10. What special services do they have?

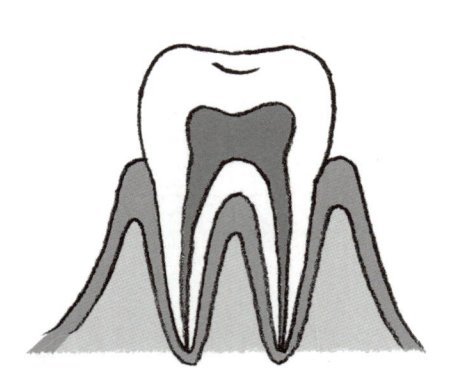

Getting Information Ⓑ

Exchange information about two dentists with your partner by asking and answering the questions below. Write the information you get in the two blank spaces. When you finish, check the information by looking at page 123. Cover your partner's page.

HAACK DENTAL CLINIC

- ❏ James Haack, D.D.S.
- ❏ Specializing in Preventive Dentistry
- ❏ 1229 West Adams Avenue
- ❏ Tel. (157) 61-1941
- ❏ Take Exit 13 off California Highway
- ❏ Appointments Preferred
- ❏ 24-hr Emergency Service
- ❏ Credit Cards Accepted
- ❏ Senior Citizen Discount

PULLUM DENTAL PLAZA

_____
_____
_____
_____
_____
_____
_____
_____
_____

CHILDREN'S DENTISTRY

_____
_____
_____
_____
_____
_____
_____

WEDRILL TEETH CARE

- ❏ Charles Wedrill, D.D.S.
- ❏ Miyoko Wedrill, D.D.S.
- ❏ 206 Old Kentucky Street
- ❏ Hrs. 9–12
- ❏ Call for Appointment
- ❏ Telephone (133) 798-8835
- ❏ Take Bus #6 to City Hall. Then Walk East 3 Blocks
- ❏ 30-Minute Teeth Cleaning

Questions:

1. What is the name of the dentist?
2. How do you spell that?
3. What is the telephone number?
4. What is the address?
5. Where, exactly, is it?
6. How do I get there?
7. Is an appointment necessary?
8. What are the hours?
9. What is their speciality?
10. What special services do they have?

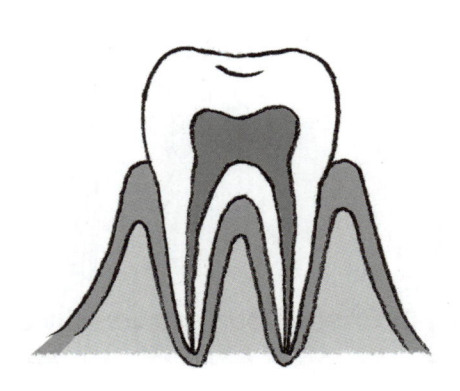

 **Dialogue Dictation** 30

Jim is explaining to Bob why he has only 30 teeth instead of the normal 32.

Jim: How ＿＿＿＿＿＿ teeth do you ＿＿＿＿＿＿?

Bob: ＿＿＿＿＿＿-＿＿＿＿＿＿. How ＿＿＿＿＿＿ you?

Jim: I ＿＿＿＿＿＿ only ＿＿＿＿＿＿.

Bob: Open your ＿＿＿＿＿＿ and ＿＿＿＿＿＿ me.

Jim: ＿＿＿＿＿＿, but ＿＿＿＿＿＿ don't ＿＿＿＿＿＿.

Bob: I ＿＿＿＿＿＿. What ＿＿＿＿＿＿ to your two ＿＿＿＿＿＿ teeth?

Jim: I had an ＿＿＿＿＿＿ with my ＿＿＿＿＿＿.

Bob: What was ＿＿＿＿＿＿ angry ＿＿＿＿＿＿?

Jim: I ＿＿＿＿＿＿ I wouldn't stop ＿＿＿＿＿＿.

Bob: Did she ＿＿＿＿＿＿ you in the ＿＿＿＿＿＿?

Jim: No. She ＿＿＿＿＿＿ an ＿＿＿＿＿＿ at me.

Bob: Then ＿＿＿＿＿＿ did ＿＿＿＿＿＿ say?

Jim: She ＿＿＿＿＿＿ that when I ＿＿＿＿＿＿ of lung ＿＿＿＿＿＿, I won't need ＿＿＿＿＿＿ anyway.

How many?

⊃ *Check your answers by using the* **Dialogue Practice** *page.*

Dialogue Practice

1. Read; 2. Remember; 3. Look Up; and 4. Speak. After you finish, change roles and do it again.

A

Jim: How **many** teeth do you **have**?

Bob: ....

Jim: I **have** only **30**.

Bob: ....

Jim: **Okay**, but **please** don't **laugh**.

Bob: ....
....

Jim: I had an **argument** with my **wife**.

Bob: ....

Jim: I **said** I wouldn't stop **smoking**.

Bob: ....

Jim: No. She **threw** an **ashtray** at me.

Bob: ....

Jim: She **said** that when I **die** of lung **cancer**, I won't need **teeth** anyway.

B

Jim: ....

Bob: **Thirty-two**. How **about** you?

Jim: ....

Bob: Open your **mouth** and **show** me.

Jim: ....

Bob: I **see**. What **happened** to your two **front** teeth?

Jim: ....

Bob: What was **she** angry **about**?

Jim: ....

Bob: Did she **punch** you in the **mouth**?

Jim: ....

Bob: Then **what** did **she** say?

Jim: ....
....

 # You and Your Partner

Exchange information about dental care with your partner. First, answer the questions for yourself.

● Cleaning

You	Partner

1. How often do you brush your teeth?
2. Do you use a fluoride toothpaste?
3. Do you use a soft toothbrush?
4. Do you use dental floss?

● Nutrition

You	Partner

5. Do you eat a lot of sweet foods?
6. What is your favorite snack?
7. How much milk do you drink?
8. Do you smoke?

● Dentist

You	Partner

9. Do you get regular checkups?
10. When was the last one you had?
11. How many teeth do you have?
12. How many fillings do you have?

I think my teeth-care habits are: (circle one)

1. VERY GOOD   **2.** GOOD   **3.** AVERAGE   **4.** POOR

What things can you do to improve them?

 **Read This**

Good for Teeth or Bad for Teeth?

Seventy percent of all Japanese eat snacks between meals, according to a survey. This isn't a bad habit as long as you eat the right kind of snacks.

But many people eat the wrong snacks because 90 percent of processed snacks contain sugar—either in its processed form as in cookies, or in its natural form as in orange juice.

It helps to brush your teeth after eating snacks, but most people don't do it.

The chart below shows some snacks that are good for you (right), and some that are not (left).

 CAVITY STARTERS
- Cookies and Candy
- Regular Soft Drinks
- Chewing Gum, Pudding
- Citrus Fruits, Juices
- Honey, Ice Cream, Pie

 CAVITY STOPPERS
- Natural Cheese, Nuts
- Raw Vegetables
- Strawberries, Apples
- Popcorn, Crackers
- Plain Yogurt, Milk

What other foods can you think of to add to this list? Write three items for each category in the chart below.

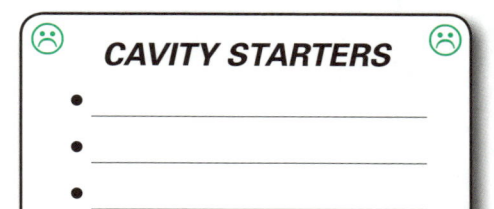 **CAVITY STARTERS**
- _____
- _____
- _____

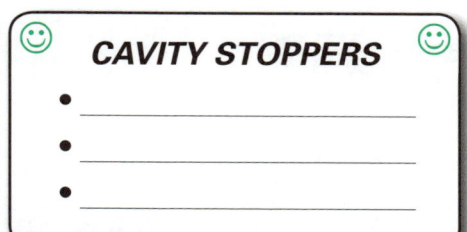 **CAVITY STOPPERS**
- _____
- _____
- _____

What is your favorite CAVITY STARTER? _____

What is your favorite CAVITY STOPPER? _____

 **Listening for Content** 31

Read, listen, and then write to complete the sentences.

The Importance of Dental Floss

Flossing your teeth is as important as brushing them. Dental floss is popular in the U.S.A., but, unfortunately, many Japanese don't know what dental floss is.

1. A _____ can _____ the _____ surface, but

it _____ clean _____ the _____.

2. The _____ of _____ floss is to _____

between the _____.

3. Dental _____ is a thin, _____ thread made of

_____ or plastic.

4. It helps _____ gum disease by removing _____ and

plaque from _____ the teeth.

5. There are _____ kinds of dental floss _____.

6. A _____ showed that _____ flossing can help you

_____ longer.

How to Floss

John & John
WAXED
(10yd)

Standard Type   **Soft-Picks**   **Floss-Pick**

Activities for Conversation Practice

A Agree or Disagree

What is your opinion of the following statement? Make notes in the appropriate box and get ready to give your reasons when asked by your teacher or your partner.

Fluoride should be put in Japanese water to prevent cavities.

AGREE

DISAGREE

B Create a Dialogue

One student be A and the other be B. Work together and write out five exchanges of at least five words each. Practice; then do the dialogue in front of the class.

1. **A** is worried about his teeth, so he wants to eat only snacks that have no sugar. **B** is giving **A** advice about what snacks are good for his teeth.

2. **A**, a high school boy, can't decide whether to become a dentist or a doctor. **B**, his teacher, tells him why becoming a dentist would be better.

3. **A** doesn't know what fluoride and dental floss are. He asks **B**, and **B** explains to him.

C Topics for Discussion and Writing

Individual and group. Write out your answers for the following questions, then discuss them with your classmates.

1. Fluoride and dental floss are popular in the U.S. for cavity prevention, but many Japanese do not use them. Why do you think this is so?

2. Most people take better care of their hair than they do their teeth. Why do you think this is so?

3. What kind of dental problems have you had?

Public Health Center

🎧 32

The AIDS Crisis Concerns Everyone

Seventy million people will die before an AIDS cure is found, according to AIDS experts. Seventy million! Some of this number will be in Japan. Could you be one of them? Possibly you could. Even if you don't get AIDS, the economic impact of the global AIDS epidemic will affect

5 you in the future. Any way you look at it, AIDS is something you should know about and be concerned about.

AIDS stands for Acquired Immune Deficiency Syndrome, which is the name given to a group of illnesses caused by a virus. The virus is called Human Immunodeficiency Virus, or HIV. The disease is considered fatal;

10 that is, HIV in a person usually develops into AIDS after a number of years, and this usually leads to death because there is no cure.

Once a person is infected with the HIV virus, it travels through the body attacking the immune system. The immune system is the body's way of protecting itself against harmful germs and infections. Since the

15 virus works by attacking the immune cells that are supposed to protect

our bodies, finding a cure is very difficult.

HIV is an unusual virus because a person can be infected for many years, yet appear to be perfectly healthy. Eventually, however, the virus multiplies inside the body and destroys the body's ability to fight off illnesses, even simple infections like the common cold. 20

The main way in which a young person in Japan can become infected with HIV is this: by having sexual intercourse with an infected partner. The virus is present in the sexual fluids and blood of infected people. If infected blood or fluid gets into your blood, then you will become infected. You can avoid becoming infected in three ways: (1) Abstain from sex, that 25 is, no sex; (2) Have sex only with a partner you are certain is not infected; (3) Use a condom each time you have sex. Condoms are effective only if used correctly, and they are not 100 percent safe because they can break.

Each year, thousands of young people in Japan donate blood. And, each year a growing number of them are shocked to find out they have 30 the HIV virus. They probably thought, "It can't happen to me." That way of thinking is wrong. Although the official number of infected people in Japan is low compared to other countries, that number is just the "tip of the iceberg." In other words, there are probably thousands in Japan who are infected but don't know it. If you think you could be infected, you 35 should get a checkup—a simple blood test—as soon as possible. These tests are free and anonymous at public health centers throughout Japan. Sooner is better than later because if a person gets treatment early, he or she can live longer.

Your behavior is the key. You can reduce the risk of AIDS infection by 40 avoiding risky activities. Having sex without a condom with a number of different partners increases your chances of getting infected. Another behavior to avoid is heavy drinking. Drinking impairs judgment, and young people are less likely to practice safe sex when they are drunk.

The AIDS epidemic is spreading all over the world, and the number of 45 people infected is constantly increasing, even in Japan. You can fight AIDS by knowing about it, practicing safe sex, and keeping a prejudice-free attitude towards those who have the disease.

Five Questions Plus One

Answer the five questions. Then, make a question to be written on the blackboard for the class to answer.

① How many people are expected to die from AIDS before a cure is found?

② Why is HIV an unusual virus?

③ What is the main way in which a young person in Japan can become infected?

④ How can being drunk increase your chances of getting AIDS?

⑤ How can you fight AIDS?

Plus One

Your Question: _____

The Answer: _____

True or False Questions

Circle T (True) or F (False) for each statement. If the statement is False, correct it to make it True.

T F **1.** The AIDS virus travels through the body and attacks the body's immune system.

T F **2.** To abstain from an activity means to not do it.

T F **3.** If you use a condom during sex, you don't have to worry about AIDS because condoms are 100 percent safe.

T F **4.** If you have sex without a condom with many different sexual partners, you increase the chances of getting infected with HIV.

T F **5.** The number of HIV-positive people in Japan is probably many times more than the known figure.

Using Key Words Correctly

Write the missing word in each sentence by choosing a word from the WORD LIST below. Use your glossary if necessary.

1. When something affects everyone around the world, it is called

   _____.

2. _____ is caused by a virus called _____.

3. A _____ accident or illness results in death.

4. To become _____ means to get a disease or illness.

5. To _____ something means to give it to a charity or an organization without getting paid for it.

6. A _____ activity is one that may be dangerous to your health.

7. To feel _____ means to have an unreasonable or unfair dislike of someone or something.

8. The physical act of sex between two people is called _____.

9. If something lowers or damages your ability to make good decisions, then we can say that it _____ judgment.

10. An _____ test is one in which you do not have to give your name, address, or telephone number.

WORD LIST		
• fatal	• impairs	• donate
• global	• prejudice	• risky
• infected	• AIDS	• HIV
• anonymous	• sexual intercourse	

Getting Information Ⓐ

How much do you know about AIDS? First, answer the seven questions in this AIDS QUIZ by circling a, b, or c. Then, check your answers by asking your partner the question and listening to his answer. Do not look at your partner's page.

Q=Question for you to answer   **A**=The answer to B's question

1. Q: The earliest known case of AIDS was in what year?
   a. 1959 **b.** 1968 **c.** 1982

  A: AIDS was first recognized as a major disease in 1982.

2. Q: Where is AIDS thought to have originated?
   a. Asia **b.** U.S.A **c.** Africa

  A: It was first confirmed in Japan in 1985.

3. Q: Who is most likely to get AIDS?
   a. men
   b. women
   c. equal chance

  A: It means Sexually Transmitted Disease.

4. Q: How long can a person–if untreated–be infected without showing symptoms?
   a. 1 year–2 years.
   b. 5–12 years.
   c. 20–25 years.

  A: They got AIDS by receiving infected blood transfusions.

5. Q: What protects you the most against HIV?
   a. vitamins
   b. birth control pills
   c. condoms

  A: No, it does not mostly affect gay people.

6. Q: What color is the AIDS awareness ribbon?
   a. blue **b.** red **c.** green

  A: It is held on December 1.

7. Q: Where are HIV tests free in Japan?
   a. private clinics
   b. public hospitals
   c. public health centers

  A: Little progress is being made in the search for a cure.

● Rate Yourself ●
6–7 correct:
  You know a lot about AIDS.
4–5 correct:
  You know a little about AIDS.
0–3 correct:
  You don't know enough about AIDS.

Getting Information Ⓑ

How much do you know about AIDS? First, answer the seven questions in this AIDS QUIZ by circling a, b, or c. Then, check your answers by asking your partner the question and listening to his answer. Do not look at your partner's page.

Q=Question for you to answer   **A**=The answer to A's question

1. Q: When was AIDS first recognized as a major disease?
a. 1954 **b.** 1967 **c.** 1982

A: The earliest known case of AIDS was in 1959.

2. Q: When was the first case of AIDS confirmed in Japan?
a. 1975 **b.** 1985 **c.** 1995

A: AIDS is thought to have originated in Africa.

3. Q: AIDS is primarily an STD. What is STD?
a. special treatment disease
b. standard testing device
c. sexually transmitted disease

A: Both men and women have an equal chance of getting AIDS.

4. Q: In Japan, in the late 1980s, how did a certain group of people contact AIDS?
a. from gay sex
b. by taking illegal drugs
c. blood transfusions

A: AIDS symptoms may not appear for 5–12 years after infection.

5. Q: Does HIV/AIDS mostly affect gay people?
a. yes **b.** no **c.** mostly gay men

A: The best protection against HIV infection is condoms.

6. Q: When is World AIDS Day held?
a. January 1
b. June 1
c. December 1

A: The AIDS awareness ribbon is red.

7. Q: How much progress is being made in the search for an AIDS cure?
a. little progress
b. good progress
c. great progress

A: They are free at public health centers.

●**Rate Yourself**●
6–7 correct:
You know a lot about AIDS.
4–5 correct:
You know a little about AIDS.
0–3 correct:
You don't know enough about AIDS.

Dialogue Dictation 🎧 33

Kenji is a 27-year-old salaryman who is getting married in a few days. He is talking to an insurance agent about buying life insurance.

Kenji: How _____ does it take to _____ a new life _____ policy?

Agent: It takes a _____ because you have to get a _____ test for HIV.

Kenji: HIV? _____ is that?

Agent: It's the _____ that causes _____.

Kenji: I don't need the _____. I couldn't have AIDS because the only person I have _____ with is my _____.

Agent: Why are you so _____ she _____ have AIDS?

Kenji: Because she is a _____ girl, a very _____ person.

Agent: That doesn't _____. Nice girls and nice _____ get AIDS, too. Do you know her sexual _____?

Kenji: Well, not _____. Should I _____ her?

Agent: No, just _____ the test. All insurance _____ require it.

Kenji: What if I don't _____ the test?! Oh, _____! I should have been more _____!

⊃ *Check your answers by using the Dialogue Practice page.*

Dialogue Practice

I. Read; 2. Remember; 3. Look Up; and 4. Speak.
After you finish, change roles and do it again.

A

Kenji: How **long** does it take to **get** a new life **insurance** policy?

Agent: ....
....

Kenji: HIV? **What** is that?

Agent: ....

Kenji: I don't need the **test**. I couldn't have AIDS because the only person I have **slept** with is my **girlfriend**.

Agent: ....
....

Kenji: Because she is a **nice** girl, a very **clean** person.

Agent: ....
....
....

Kenji: Well, not **really**. Should I **ask** her?

Agent: ....
....

Kenji: What if I don't **pass** the test? Oh, **no**! I should have been more **careful**!

B

Kenji: ....
....

Agent: It takes a **week** because you have to get a **blood** test for HIV.

Kenji: ....

Agent: It's the **virus** that causes **AIDS**.

Kenji: ....
....
....

Agent: Why are you so **sure** she **doesn't** have AIDS?

Kenji: ....
....

Agent: That doesn't **matter**. Nice girls and nice **boys** get AIDS, too. Do you know her sexual **history**?

Kenji: ....

Agent: No, just **take** the test. All insurance **companies** require it.

Kenji: ....
....

 # You and Your Partner

How Is HIV/AIDS Transmitted?

AIDS is a terrible disease, but, fortunately, it is not easily transmitted by everyday activities.

This chart shows some ways that the disease can and cannot be transmitted. It shows the likelihood of infection by various activities, assuming the is present. (Note: These are generalizations.)

Study the chart, then ask each other questions based on the sample sentences below. One student take the even questions, and the other student take the odd questions.

KEY **E**=Easy to transmit   **D**=Difficult to transmit   **I**=Impossible to transmit

Activity	E	D	I
① Blood transfusions	○		
② Normal kissing			○
③ Vaginal intercourse	○		
④ Coughing in a person's face			○
⑤ Deep kissing		○	
⑥ Infected needles or syringes	○		
⑦ Pregnant woman to unborn child		○	
⑧ Shaking hands			○
⑨ Toilet seats			○
⑩ Anal intercourse	○		
⑪ Mosquito bites			○
⑫ Oral sex	○		

Sample Question: Can you get HIV/AIDS from/by (_____)?

Sample Answers:

E It's easy to get HIV/AIDS from/by (_____).

D It's difficult to get HIV/AIDS from/by (_____).

I It's impossible to get HIV/AIDS from/by (_____).

# Read This

What Is Safe Sex?

Safe sex means sex which is absolutely safe. Many romantic activities are completely safe. For example, you can't get AIDS from kissing, cuddling, and massaging your partner's body.

Sex without a condom, however, is not safe. Just because your partner seems like a nice, clean person is no guarantee that he or she does not have the HIV virus. Do you really know your partner's sexual background? Most couples don't.

Oral sex (one person kissing, licking or sucking the sexual areas of another person) is not completely safe either, especially if the person has a cut or sore in the mouth or on the sexual organ.

The only 100 percent sure way to avoid AIDS is to limit your sexual activity to a partner who you know does not have the HIV virus. This means that you and your partner should have an HIV test before beginning an intimate relationship; then, avoid sex with other partners.

AIDS has made sex a little scary and more difficult these days. However, with knowledge of the disease and good judgment you can have a healthy sex life.

Choose a word below to finish the statement. Use the glossary.

1. That which is total and complete—100 percent—is (   ).
2. To (   ) means to lovingly hold someone in your arms.
3. A (   ) means that something is sure or true.
4. A (   ) is a painful place on the skin which is infected.
5. An (   ) relationship usually includes love and sex.
6. An (   ) is a part of your body that has a specific function.
7. If something is (   ), you are afraid of it.
8. A person's past personal history is his (   ).
9. We use a straw to (   ) the juice out of a glass.

a. sore	**b.** guarantee	**c.** intimate
d. absolute	**e.** cuddle	**f.** scary
g. organ	**h.** suck	**i.** background

 ## Listening for Content 34

Read, listen, and then write to complete the sentences.

The AIDS Test and How It Works

In a person who has AIDS, the body fights the virus by creating antibodies to the virus. HIV tests measure the presence of these antibodies; they do not detect the virus itself. Recently developed detection techniques include urine and saliva tests, as well as "at home" tests. However, the standard blood test is still the most widely-used method. Here is the usual procedure:

1. A person who wants to be _____ visits a medical

_____ and has a _____ sample taken.

2. The blood is _____ to determine whether or _____

HIV _____ are in it.

3. The _____ then informs the tested person whether his blood

has a _____ or _____ HIV immune _____.

4. A positive _____ means that the person has the

_____ virus.

5. It is important to _____ that it can take up to three

_____ after _____ for the HIV antibodies to

_____ in the _____.

6. Therefore, only a _____ taken

_____ months after a person's

last sexual _____ can be

_____ reliable.

 Activities for Conversation Practice

A Agree or Disagree

What is your opinion of the following statement? Make notes in the appropriate box and get ready to give your reasons when asked by your teacher or your partner.

> **Donating blood is a good way to find out if you have AIDS.**

AGREE	DISAGREE

B Create a Dialogue

One student be A and the other be B. Work together and write out five exchanges of at least five words each. Practice; then do the dialogue in front of the class.

1. **A** is trying to warn his son, **B**, about the dangers of AIDS, but **B** thinks he already knows a lot about it, and he tells his father what he knows.

2. **A** wants his friend, **B**, to go with him to get an HIV test. **B** thinks he doesn't need to worry about AIDS because he lives in Japan.

3. **A**, a hemophiliac who got AIDS from a blood transfusion, explains to **B** the discrimination he feels in society. **B** questions him about it.

C Topics for Discussion and Writing

Individual and group. Write out your answers for the following questions, then discuss them with your classmates.

1. In Japan a few years ago, a company employee was fired from his job because he tested positive for HIV. He took his case to court. If you were a judge in such a case, how would you decide? Why?

2. Discrimination against people with HIV/AIDS is still a serious problem in Japan. What do you think can be done to eliminate such prejudice?

3. In the future, how could Japan, as a rich country, be affected economically by the spread of AIDS in the poor countries?

🎧 35

Depression: Don't Let It Get You Down

One of the fastest-growing health problems in Japan today is a mental one: depression.

It is said that 1 in 5 Japanese will suffer from depression in their lifetime. In addition, over 60% of Japan's workforce is reported to be stressed or
5 depressed (stress often leads to depression). In the past, depression was not talked about because it was considered shameful to have a psychological problem. Nowadays, depression has gone from being a bad word to being a "buzzword." This means that it is now openly and often discussed.

What is depression? Known as *utsubyo* in Japanese, it is a change in
10 mood, thought and body feelings in which a person may feel sad, lonely, disappointed, hopeless, and so on. Of course, we all sometimes feel "blue" or "down." These feelings are normal. It is when such feelings become intense and long-lasting and affect our ability to do our everyday activities that we must acknowledge them and seek treatment. The causes

of depression are many: overwork, loneliness, financial trouble, weak 15
family relationships, poor communication skills, job insecurity, and more.

One student who suffered from depression described her situation
as follows: "I couldn't do homework, read a newspaper or even watch
TV. In my free time, I would just sit in a chair and look at the wall. I
couldn't sleep well, lost weight, and became angry easily. I lost interest 20
in everything." Finally, she saw a doctor who diagnosed her as having
mild depression, which is the most common type. After counseling and
getting medical treatment, her health improved.

Unlike other diseases, there is no simple test for depression. A diagnosis is made based on a person's symptoms, such as those of the student 25
mentioned above. Recognizing the problem, especially what may be
causing your problem, and getting treatment is the key.

One of the best treatments is counseling—talking about it.

Here are 6 things you can do to fight depression and keep yourself
happy every day: 30

1. CHANGE YOUR NORMAL ROUTINE. Doing the same thing
   over and over, at the same place, can be depressing.
2. BE POSITIVE, ACTIVE, & EXERCISE. Nothing improves a
   person's mood more than exercise. Sometimes just taking a walk,
   talking to a friend or going shopping can improve your mood. 35
3. REFLECT ON PAST SUCCESSES. Focus on your strong points
   and remember all the good things you have done in your life.
4. MAKE OTHERS HAPPY. This will make you happy, too. A word
   of thanks, praise, or a smile will brighten up everyone's day.
5. BE GRATEFUL FOR WHAT YOU HAVE. No matter how bad 40
   you think your situation is, there will always be other people worse
   off than you.
6. THINK ABOUT THE BIG PICTURE. Your problems are smaller
   than you think. In 100 years, no one will remember what you did
   or didn't do in your life. So, count your blessings right now and 45
   make every day a good day.

Have a goal in life, go for it, and don't let depression get you down!

Five Questions Plus One

Answer the five questions. Then, make a question to be written on the blackboard for the class to answer.

1. What is one of the fastest-growing health problems in Japan today?

2. What percentage of Japan's workforce is stressed or depressed?

3. What are some causes of depression in Japan?

4. What is one of the best treatments for depression?

5. What does exercise usually do to a person's mood?

Plus One

Your Question: _____

The Answer: _____

True or False Questions

Circle T (True) of F (False) for each statement. If the statement is False, correct it to make it True.

T   F   **1.** In the past, depression was not talked about very much.

T   F   **2.** It is not normal to sometimes feel "blue" or " down."

T   F   **3.** There are several simple tests for depression.

T   F   **4.** Most people are helped by depression treatments.

T   F   **5.** Most people think their problems are bigger than they actually are.

Matching for Understanding

Choose the expression on the right that means the same as the word on the left, as it is used in the text.

1. lifetime ( )
2. depression ( )
3. psychological ( )
4. buzzword ( )
5. blue ( )
6. treatment ( )
7. symptom ( )
8. acknowledge ( )
9. intense ( )
10. diagnosis ( )
11. respond ( )
12. blessings ( )
13. grateful ( )
14. praise ( )
15. medicine ( )

a. to feel unhappy for a short time
b. good things you are thankful for
c. to feel thanks for something
d. a sign of illness in body or mind
e. known as *utsubyo* in Japanese
f. something you take to cure illness
g. to find the cause of a sickness
h. strong, serious, extreme feeling
i. a word/expression that is popular
j. when medical treatment works
k. to accept or recognize something
l. to tell someone how good they are
m. the period from birth to death
n. concerned with a person's mind
o. medical attention for a sick person

Getting Information Ⓐ

Get information about your partner's moods and feelings. Write his/her answers in the boxes. Do not look at your partner's page.

What makes you feel down? Why?

_____
_____
_____
_____

What do you do to change your mood?

_____
_____
_____
_____

What is your best day of the week? Why?

_____
_____
_____
_____

Have you ever felt really depressed? Why?

_____
_____
_____
_____

Are you satisfied with your life? Why?

_____
_____
_____
_____

What are you most thank-ful for in life? Why?

_____
_____
_____
_____

Getting Information Ⓑ

Get information about your partner's moods and feelings. Write his/her answers in the boxes. Do not look at your partner's page.

When do you feel blue? Why?

What activity helps you change your mood?

What are your successes in life?

Do you suffer from "Blue Monday"? Why?

What was your most depressing moment? Why?

Who do you usually discuss your problems with? Why?

 **Dialogue Dictation** 36

Taro Sato (T.S.) is suffering from mild depression. He is talking to a male counselor (M.C.) about his problem, which is job-related New Type Depression.

M.C.: Please _____ in Mr. Sato. What kind of _____ are you having?

T.S.: I have been feeling really _____ and frustrated at _____. My situation is hopeless.

M.C.: What, _____, is the _____ at work?

T.S.: _____, I have not been _____ to do the work given to me by my _____.

M.C.: Have you _____ to your boss about it? I _____ he would _____ to you.

T.S.: The boss is not a "he," it is a "_____", and that is the problem. My boss is a beautiful _____ woman.

M.C.: Do you _____ you can't stop _____ at her, so you can't _____ your work done?

T.S.: No. The boss _____ me and wants to have a _____ with me, but I refused because I _____ it is not a good _____ to date the boss.

M.C.: I see. What _____ after that?

T.S.: After that, she gave me _____ work which is too _____ for me to do.

M.C.: That _____ like revenge for your _____ to have a date with her.

T.S.: I _____ so. She seems to be a very _____ girl who needs a _____.

M.C.: Well, in that _____, please come to my _____ again tomorrow—and bring me a _____ of your boss.

T.S.: What?!

Dialogue Practice

1. Read; 2. Remember; 3. Look Up; and 4. Speak. After you finish, change roles and do it again.

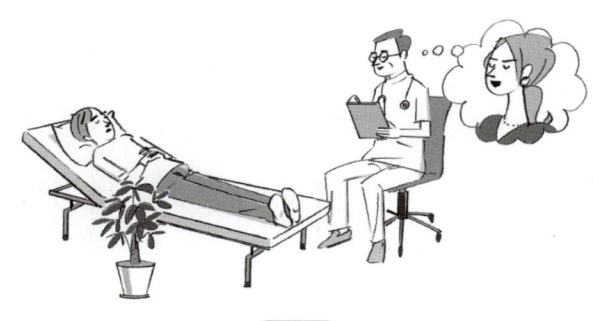

A

M.C.: Please **come** in Mr. Sato. What kind of **problem** are you having?

T.S.: ……………………………………… ………………………………………..

M.C.: What, **exactly** is the **problem** at work?

T.S.: ……………………………………… ………………………………………..

M.C.: Have you **talked** to your boss about it? I **think** he would **listen** to you.

T.S.: ……………………………………… ……………………………………….. ………………………………………..

M.C.: Do you **mean** you can't stop **looking** at her, so you can't **get** your work done?

T.S.: ……………………………………… ……………………………………….. ……………………………………….. ………………………………………..

M.C.: I see. What **happened** after that?

T.S.: ……………………………………… ………………………………………..

M.C.: That **sounds** like revenge for your **refusal** to have a date with her.

T.S.: ……………………………………… ………………………………………..

M.C.: Well in that **case**, please come to my **office** again tomorrow—and bring me a **picture** of your boss.

T.S.: ………………………………………

B

M.C.: ……………………………………… ………………………………………..

T.S.: I have been feeling really **down** and frustrated at **work.**

M.C.: ……………………………………… ………………………………………..

T.S.: **Recently**, I have not been **able** to do the work given to me by my **boss**.

M.C.: ……………………………………… ………………………………………..

T.S.: The boss is not a "he," it is a "**she**" and that is the problem. My boss is a beautiful **young** woman.

M.C.: ……………………………………… ……………………………………….. ………………………………………..

T.S.: No. The boss **likes** me and wants to have a **date** with me, but I refused because I **think** it is not a good **idea** to date the boss.

M.C.: ………………………………………

T.S.: After that, she gave me **more** work which is too **difficult** for me to do.

M.C.: ……………………………………… ………………………………………..

T.S.: I **think** so. She seems to be a very **lonely** girl who needs a **boyfriend**.

M.C.: ……………………………………… ……………………………………….. ………………………………………..

T.S.: What?

You and Your Partner

HOW HAPPY ARE YOU?

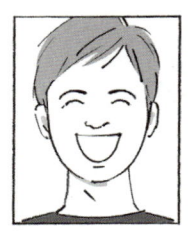

Do this happiness survey for yourself, then ask your partner the questions. Ask you partner to explain "why" after each answer.

	Yes	So-So	No
1. Are you happy most of the time?			
2. Are you proud of yourself?			
3. Are you successful at most things?			
4. Do you have a clear purpose in life?			
5. Are you thankful for what you have?			
6. Do you love and trust other people?			
7. Are you satisfied with your present situation?			
8. Do you laugh a lot?			
9. Can you easily get over a bad mood?			
10. Do you have a lot of good friends?			
11. Do you avoid worrying about small things?			
12. Do you sleep well and feel energetic?			
13. Are you happy with your physical appearance?			
14. Do you feel in control of your life?			
15. Are you optimistic about the future?			

Rate Your Happiness Level: On a scale of 5 to 1, with 5 being "very happy" and 1 being "very unhappy" circle your rating: 5 4 3 2 1

What is one important thing that would help to improve your happiness level? Can you explain why?

Read This

9-to-5 Depression

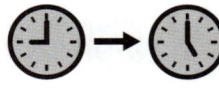

Depression in the workplace is a growing problem in Japan. It is caused by rising job insecurity and workplace changes resulting from Japan's economic decline.

This on-the-job depression is also called New Type Depression (NTD), and it is most common among workers in their 20s and 30s. The main causes are criticism from the boss, communication problems, and failure to do the job as expected.

A key feature of NTD is that these workers become depressed only at work; outside of work they are able to enjoy their private time normally. When depressed employees can not do their work well, Japan's economic productivity suffers.

Here are some NTD facts For Japan:

- The number of people suffering from NTD has increased to over one million.
- Over 80% of businesses say problems of mental health affect their business performance negatively.
- More than 30% of businesses say they have cases of workers quitting or unable to work because of NTD
- The weakening of the system of older workers helping younger workers is one cause of the increase of NTD.
- There is a close relationship between NTD and suicide.

From the reading above, <u>underline</u> the correct answer in each sentence.

1. Workplace depression in Japan is **increasing/decreasing**.
2. These days, the loss of job **security/insecurity** worries many workers.
3. NTD affects mostly **younger/older** workers.
4. What makes NTD different from ordinary depression is the **place/season** it occurs.
5. People suffering from NTD usually feel **depressed/fine** athome.
6. The senior-junior, *senpai-kohai* system is **still strong/weakening**.
7. Severe cases of NTD may result in people killing **themselves/their co-workers**.

Diagnosing Depression

Everybody has days when they feel some sadness because life is full of ups and downs. Usually, these feelings go away after a few days.

Depression, on the other hand, continues on for weeks or months. It affects your mood and thoughts and prevents you from enjoying daily life. It is not easy to understand or diagnose.

Here are some of the classic symptoms and examples of depression:

1. *Difficulty Concentrating:* When you try to _____, your mind continually wanders and you can not _____ on the _____.

2. *Short-term Memory Loss:* You are _____ forgetting _____ you used to be able to _____ easily.

3. *Pessimism:* You think _____ and believe that only _____ things are going to happen.

4. *Loss of Enjoyment:* The things you used to _____ doing are no longer _____ to do.

5. *Fatigue & Aches and Pains:* You have no _____ and feel physically _____.

6. *Anger and Irritability:* You get easily _____ about things that never _____ you before.

7. *Changes in Appetite & Weight:* You don't feel like _____ the things you used to _____, and you lose weight or you _____ and gain weight.

8. *Difficulty Sleeping:* Your sleeping _____ have become _____.

9. *Problems at Work or School:* You can not do your _____ or school work _____.

If some of these symptoms continue for several weeks, you may be suffering from depression!

Activities for Conversation Practice

A Agree or Disagree

What is your opinion of the following statement? Make notes in the appropriate box and get ready to give your reasons when asked by your teacher or your partner.

Women get depressed more easily than men.

AGREE	DISAGREE

B Create a Dialogue

One student be A and the other be B. Work together and write out five exchanges of at least five words each. Practice; then do the dialogue in front of the class.

1. **A** thinks he might be suffering from NTD at work. His friend, **B**, understands NTD and explains to him what it is.

2. **A** tells his friend, **B**, that he wants to take a depression test. **B** explains that there is no simple test for depression. Then **B** explains some of the signs of depression.

3. **A** is feeling down because his girlfriend left him. **B** tries to find out why **A**'s girlfriend left him and gives advice on how to get her back.

C Topics for Discussion and Writing

Individual and group. Write out your answers for the following questions, then discuss them with your classmates.

1. The expression "kokoro no kaze" was introduced by the Japanese drug industry to explain mild depression. How would you explain this expression in English?

2. NTD is more common among younger workers than older workers. Why do you think this condition affects mostly younger people?

3. Many Japanese who have depression follow the KITY rule (Keep it to yourself.) Do you think this is a good idea or not? Why?

English-Japanese Glossary

＊動詞以外は，原則としてできるだけテキストに出てくる形で表してある。

A

ability 能力 35
abnormal 異常な 17
abstain 控える 123
accident 事故 75
accidental 思いがけない 34
according to …によれば 119
ache 痛み 144
acids 酸 111
acknowledge 認める 134
activity 活動 5
add 加える 3
addiction 中毒になって 27
adjustment 調節 6
adult 大人の 99
aerobic エアロビクスの 51
affect 影響する 45
agree 同意する 9
air 空気，大気 7
airline ticket 航空券 109
alcoholic アルコール中毒の 74
alcoholism アルコール中毒 74
alike よく似ている 63
although …だけれども 2
amazing すごい 81
ambitious 大望を抱いた 90
amount 量 3
anal 肛門の 130
anonymous 匿名の 123
anorexia 拒食症 107
anyway いずれにしろ 68
appetite 食欲 144
appliances 家電 39
appointment 予約 114
approximate おおよその 12
artificial chemicals 人工的な化学薬
品 38
as long as …でさえあれば 119
asbestos アスベスト 42
assessment 査定、アセスメント 46
asthma 喘息 38
at least 少なくとも 3
attention 注意 22
available 利用できる 98
average 平均的な；平均して…となる 3
avoid 避ける 3

B

background 背景 2
bacteria 細菌 29
baldness はげていること 95
based on …に基づいて 59
basement 地階 114
basically 基本的には 74
behavior 行動 3
bet 賭け 8
bite かむ 113
bladder 膀胱 95
bleeding 出血 83
blessings 祝福、恩恵 135
block （市街地の）一区画 114
blood pressure 血圧 34
blood transfusion 輸血 126
bodily 身体の 87
boil 沸騰させる 39
bone 骨 11
boring 退屈な 51
brain 脳 3
brand 銘柄 30
breast 乳房 15
breathe 呼吸する 27
brush ブラシで磨く 111
bull horns 拡声器 39

burn 燃やす *52*
butts たばこの吸い殻 *27*

C

caffeine カフェイン *71*
calorie カロリー *3*
can 缶詰 *70*
cancer がん *3*
capacity 容量 *11*
carbohydrates 炭水化物 *63*
carbon monoxide 一酸化炭素 *27*
carcinogens 発がん物質 *36*
care about 関心を持つ *3*
case 事例, 場合 *24*
cause 引き起こす;原因 *2*
cavity 空洞 *113*
cells 細胞 *11*
central nervous system 中枢神経
　系 *27*
cerebellum 小脳 *83*
certain ある一定の *2*
charity 慈善団体 *125*
checkup 検査 *111*
chemical 化学薬品 *17*
chemotherapy 化学療法 *20*
chew かむ *110*
cholesterol コレステロール *12*
choose 選ぶ *7*
cilia 繊毛 *35*
cirrhosis 肝硬変 *83*
citrus 柑橘類の *119*
climate change 気候変動 *38*
clearly 明らかに *15*
clerk 職員 *109*
climb 登る *50*
colleagues 同僚 *74*
collect たまる *111*
colon 結腸 *15*
combine 結合する *110*
comfortable 快適な *87*
compare 比較する *97*
competition 試合 *61*
composter コンポスター *39*
condition 状態 *50*

confuse 混乱させる *13*
consider 考えてみる *3*
construction material 建築資材 *42*
consumption 消費 *39*
contain 含む *27*
cooperative 協力的な *90*
cope うまく処理をする *75*
copper 銅 *42*
coronary heart trouble 冠状動脈の病
　気 *99*
correct 訂正する *40*
cough せき *22*
court 裁判所 *133*
crazy （頭が）おかしい *57*
create 作る *13*
criticism 批判 *143*
cross-country 山野を横断する *61*
crush つぶす *113*
cuddle 抱き締める *131*
cure 回復させる;治療法 *17*
cured food 保存食 *15*
custom 習慣 *47*
customer 顧客 *47*
cut down 量を減らす *42*
cute かわいらしい *94*
cyanide シアン化合物 *27*

D

daily life 日常生活 *15*
dairy products 乳製品 *15*
dangerous 危険な *17*
deadly 致命的な *27*
decay 腐敗 *110*
decide 決心する *18*
decision 決定 *77*
decrease 減少する *35*
delicious おいしい *62*
dental care 歯の管理 *110*
dental floss デンタルフロス *111*
dentist 歯科医 *110*
depend on …による *15*
depression 憂鬱な *27*
desire 願望 *7*
detect 見つける *132*

fresh-grown 新鮮な *63*
front teeth 前歯 *117*
frustrated 落胆した、不満を抱いた *140*
fuel 燃料 *39*
future 未来；将来の *10*

G

garbage ゴミ *38*
gender 性（の区分）*2*
germs 細菌 *29*
glue 接着剤 *113*
go together 調和する *76*
government 政府 *47*
graduate 卒業生；卒業する *5*
gram-for-gram 量が同じなら *75*
grateful 感謝して *135*
greenhouse gases 温室効果ガス *38*
gum disease 歯ぐきの病気 *110*

H

habits 習慣 *45*
hair loss 抜け毛 *87*
harm 害する *29*
harmful 有害な *29*
heal 治る *17*
health awareness 健康に対する意識 *iv*
heart 心臓 *3*
heart attack 心臓麻痺 *6*
heart disease 心臓病 *3*
heat waves 気象熱波 *38*
heavy drinkers 大酒飲み *75*
height 身長 *106*
helpless どうしようもない *14*
hemophiliac 血友病患者 *133*
high blood pressure 高血圧 *75*
high-fiber foods 高繊維食品 *15*
hit 殴る *85*
hoarseness かすれ声 *22*
honest 正直な *90*
honey 蜂蜜 *119*
hours 診療時間 *114*
human resources 人的資源 *86*
hurt 傷つける *88*

I

ideal 理想的な *98*
illegally 不法に *41*
illness 病気 *75*
imagine 想像する *74*
immediately すぐさま *22*
immune system 免疫系統 *11*
impair 損なう *123*
important 重要な *14*
impossible 不可能な *81*
import 輸入する *39*
improve 向上させる，改善する *39*
inactive 活動しない *50*
include 含む *15*
including …を含めて *54*
increase 増加する *3*
indicate 示す *5*
indigestion 消化不良 *22*
individual 個人；個人の *13*
infection 感染 *35*
information 情報 *5*
insects 昆虫 *41*
insecurity 不安定 *135*
insurance 保険 *20*
intake 摂取量 *72*
intense （感情・行動などが）激しい、真剣な *134*
international 国際的な *61*
intestine 腸 *83*
intimate 親密な *131*
introduce 紹介する *104*
irritable 怒りっぽい *27*
irritation 痛み，炎症 *95*
item 品目 *70*

J

jingle 響きのよい詩句 *73*
judge 裁判官 *133*
judgment 判断 *29*
junk food 即席食品やファーストフードなど栄養に欠ける食品 *3*

nowadays 今日では *75*
nutrition 栄養, 栄養学 *62*
nutritious 栄養のある *63*
nylon string ナイロン糸 *111*

O

oatmeal オートミール *15*
obese 肥満した *18*
obesity 肥満 *2*
obvious 明らかな *22*
occur 生じる *23*
oil spills 石油流出 *42*
on-the-run 多忙で *63*
only child ひとりっ子 *94*
openly 公然と *37*
optimistic 楽観的な *142*
oral 口腔の *11*
organically-grown 有機栽培の *39*
organisms 生物 *113*
organs 臓器 *29*
outer surface 外側の表面 *111*
overweight 太りすぎ *6*

P

pace 速度, ペース *87*
pack 一箱 *6*
pain 痛み *22*
palm reading 手相 *10*
partner 相手 *10*
pass air 空気を送り込む *7*
pastime 気晴らし *75*
patient 患者；辛抱強い *90*
performance 機能 *51*
period 期間 *51*
personal 個人的な *86*
personality 性格 *2*
pessimism 悲観 *144*
pesticide-laced 殺虫剤を加えた *38*
physical 身体の *5*
piles 積み重ね *38*
plain 普通の *71*
plaque 歯垢 *110*
pleasures 喜び *62*
plenty of たくさんの *15*

poach ゆでる *107*
poisonous 有害な *26*
positive 積極的な *3*
posture 姿勢 *11*
praise 賞賛する *137*
precious 貴重な *39*
predict 予言する *10*
preferred 望ましい *115*
pregnant 妊娠した *130*
prejudice 偏見 *123*
preservation 保存 *63*
prevent 防ぐ *4*
price to pay 代償 *63*
prison 刑務所 *97*
probably たぶん *24*
processed 加工した *99*
processing 加工 *17*
produce …を引き起こす *41*
productivity 生産性 *143*
products 製品 *12*
proper 正しい *52*
prostate 前立腺 *15*
protein 蛋白質 *63*
provide 与える *74*
psychological 精神の、心理学的な *134*
psychologist 心理学者 *97*
pulse rate 脈拍数 *34*
pumping power 血液を送る能力 *11*
punch 殴る *117*
pure 混じりけのない *39*
purpose 目的 *142*

Q

quality 質, 特性 *2*
questionnaire アンケート用紙 *5*
quit やめる *27*

R

radiation 放射線 *23*
rain forests （熱帯）雨林 *38*
rapid 速い *75*
rash 発疹 *95*
raw 生の *70*
reactions 反応 *75*

recent 最近の *42*

recently 最近 *99*

redistribute 区分し直す *11*

reduce 減らす *15*

reflect 再考する *135*

refresh …を新鮮にする *87*

regular 定期的な *111*

regularly 定期的に *7*

related 関係のある *14*

relax くつろがせる *74*

reliable 確かな *132*

relief 軽減, 除去 *3*

rely 頼る *39*

remove 取り除く *111*

repair 修理する *39*

replace …に取って代わる *23*

reproductive organs 生殖器官 *95*

require 必要とする *3*

required 必要とされる *114*

researcher 研究者 *7*

resistance training ウェイトトレーニング *107*

respond 答える *137*

resources 資源 *41*

result （…から）生じる；結果 *24*

rewrite …を書き直す *4*

risk 危険 *25*

risk factor 危険な要因 *111*

romantic ロマンチックな *85*

rotten 腐った *113*

rough きめの粗い *11*

rubbish ゴミ *29*

S

sailor 船乗り *73*

saliva 唾液 *132*

salting 塩漬けにすること *17*

scare 怖がらせる *14*

scary 怖い *110*

science 科学 *59*

scientists 科学者 *2*

scold しかる *37*

seatbelt シートベルト *3*

secretly 内緒で *37*

seek 求める *22*

select 選ぶ *53*

self-confidence 自信 *3*

self-control 自己管理 *99*

selfish わがままな *90*

senses 感覚 *29*

sensitive 気にする *95*

shameful 恥ずかしい *134*

shape （健康などの）状態 *50*

shelter 避難所 *41*

shoreline 海岸線 *42*

shout どなる *89*

shy 内気な *47*

simple 容易な *3*

situation 状態 *39*

skin 皮膚 *11*

skinny やせ（こけ）た *107*

skip 抜く, 省く *18*

slender すらりとした *107*

slim ほっそりした *107*

slow 衰えさせる *83*

smart 利口な *10*

smell においがする *27*

smoke 喫煙する *3*

smoking (meat) （肉を）薫製にすること *17*

snack 間食をとる *98*

snacks 間食 *108*

society 社会, 会 *3*

soft drink 清涼飲料 *71*

soil 土壌 *41*

sore 痛み, 痛む個所 *22*

special 特製の *69*

specialist 専門家 *99*

speciality 専門 *114*

spinach ホウレンソウ *73*

spread 広がる *17*

stain しみをつける, 汚す *34*

stairs 階段 *50*

statement 陳述 *4*

stay …であり続ける *98*

sticky ねばねばする *110*

stiffness 堅いこと *51*

stimulate 刺激する *27*

stomach 胃 15
stoop 腰が曲がる 11
strange 変な，妙な 8
stress relief ストレスの解消 27
stressful ストレスの多い 18
substance 物質 27
subtract 引く 5
success 成功 2
suck 吸う 131
suffer （苦痛などを）受ける 34
suicide 自殺 86
superior 優れた 59
surface 表面 111
surgery 手術 23
surprised 驚いた 20
survey 調査 47
sustain 維持する 38
swallow 飲み込む 22
symptom 兆候 111
syringes 注射器 130

T

talkative おしゃべりな 90
tar タール 29
tartar 歯石 111
taste …の味がする 3
temperature 体温 35
temporary 一時的な 75
tendency 傾向 106
tension 緊張 75
therefore 従って 2
thin 細い 107
thought 思考 75
threat 脅威 41
threw 投げた 85
throat のど 34
tightness 固いこと 95
timber 材木 41
timetable 予定表 53
tiny ごく小さい 23
tip of the iceberg 氷山の一角 123
toilet habits トイレの習慣（一日に行く 回数など） 22
tongue 舌 111

tooth decay 虫歯 110
toothpaste 練り歯磨き 111
toxic chemicals 有害化学物質 41
trading company 貿易商社 86
traditional 伝統的な，昔風の 63
trainer トレーナー 61
transmit 伝染させる 126
trap わなをかける 27
trash ゴミ 39
treat 治療する 23
treatments 治療 21
typical 典型的な 94

U

ulcers 潰瘍 34
underweight 体重不足の 106
unfortunately 残念ながら 3
unhealthy 健康によくない 2
unnecessary 不必要な 63
unusual bleeding 異常出血 22
unwilling 気が進まない 53
upset 調子を悪くする，狼狽した 71
urine 尿 71

V

vagina 膣 130
value 価値 7
variety of いろいろな 63
vending machines 自動販売機 42
vicious circle 悪循環 27
victims 犠牲者 86
viruses ビールス 36
vital 不可欠な 41
vitamins ビタミン 63

W

wander 迷う 144
warning labels 警告ラベル 13
warning signs 徴候 22
wart いぼ 22
waste 浪費 38
wear 摩滅する 7
wear out 疲れ切らせる，使い古す 7
weigh …の重さがある 71

HEALTHTALK
Health Awareness & English Conversation
NEW EDITION
● 健康を英語で考える・改訂新版 ●

2019 年 1 月 20 日　初版発行
2022 年 2 月 17 日　初版 2 刷

著　者　Bert McBean
発行者　秦　隆司
発行所　株式会社　トライアログ・エデュケーション
　　　　〒 167-0051 東京都杉並区荻窪 4–28–11
　　　　電話 03-6383-5991　　FAX 0120-953-514
　　　　http://www.tryalogue.co.jp/
　　　　E-mail: contact@tryalogue.co.jp
発売元　株式会社　シェーンコーポレーション ネリーズ事業部
　　　　https://nellies-bs.com/
　　　　E-mail: shoten@nellies.jp

印刷・製本／株式会社エデュプレス
編集／株式会社オフィス LEPS
本文イラスト／おぐらきょうこ
DTP・カバーデザイン／有限会社ザイン